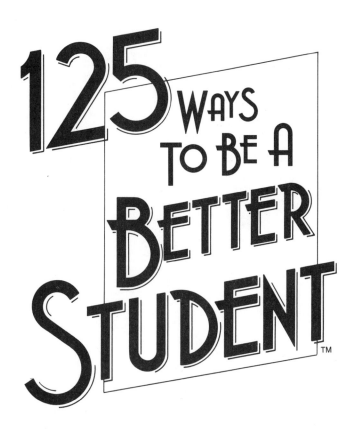

125 WAYS TO BE A BETTER STUDENT

Authors: Paula Currie
           Mary T deBrueys
           Jill Exnicios
           Marsha Prejean

LinguiSystems ®

LinguiSystems, Inc.
3100 4th Avenue
East Moline, IL 61244

1-800-PRO IDEA
1-800-776-4332

Skill Area:	Study Skills
Interest Level:	5th grade thru Adult
Reading Level:	3.5 thru 4.5

Printed in the U.S.A.
ISBN 1-55999-063-5

Preface

---

125 Ways to Be a Better Student is a compilation of several years of hands-on experience with students in the areas of organization and study skills. *125 Ways to Be a Better Student* is intended for teachers and students whose goal is to enhance these skills. After learning the purpose and procedure of each skill, and receiving specific guidelines, students apply each skill through practical activities.

March 1987

Paula Currie
Mary T deBrueys
Jill Exnicios
Marsha Prejean

Table of Contents

Introduction

Students with weak organizational and study skills do exist — both among the language-learning disordered population and the population not affected by such disorders. This book is designed to meet the needs of such students, whether seen individually or in group or classroom situations.

125 Ways to Be a Better Student is arranged in one complete book, to facilitate use by instructors. Practical information and guidelines, as well as worksheet example answers, are provided for instructors.

It is important for instructors using this book to understand the comprehensive scope of study skills. While this text lends itself to teaching individual units based on need or classroom circumstance, using the book as a whole and incorporating all study skills in an organized fashion over time will be most beneficial to students. When used as a whole program, the study skills in this book enhance organization, independence, and the ability to study in all academic situations. It is important to make every effort to enable students to realize the importance of these skills and to apply these skills to daily academics. The handouts and student worksheets are ideal for students' reference throughout their academic years.

ORGANIZING YOURSELF AND YOUR STUDY TIME

How do your students plan and use their study time? The way students plan and use study time often reveals how organized they are. This unit gives your students several helpful strategies on how to organize and plan ahead efficiently.

2 handouts (pages 12-15)
3 worksheets (pages 16-18)

Begin this unit by asking your students what they think organizing themselves means. Discuss their answers and put them on the board or an overhead. Help generate discussion regarding the importance of self organizing by asking them where, when, and how they study best. Some students will study right after school. Others need a break. Some study best at a desk. Others may work best at a table with a large surface area. Some students require a quiet place for study. Others find that soft music helps them to concentrate. Some students study best alone, and some study better with help from someone else. Suggest these ideas if your students need help with this brainstorming.

Next, read and discuss the handouts with your students. These handouts contain eleven easy-to-achieve, success-oriented goals. If your students realize that these goals will help them get organized, and that better organization means better learning, better grades, and

more free time, they'll work harder to achieve these goals.

Finally, introduce the worksheets. Encourage your students to discuss the questions with friends or family. Then, discuss the worksheets with your students. Help them choose ways to modify their study routines based on the problem solving they do, and on their individual needs.

Relating this new skill of "organizing yourself" to a skill your students already have would be an ideal learning facilitator. Perhaps you know enough about each one of your students to relate the skill of self-organizing to a skill they each already possess. However you present this material, feel free to expand upon or delete material, as necessary, to meet individual needs. We know how difficult it is for us to get organized. Imagine the struggle our students have! Good luck, and good organization!

Handout: *6 Ways to Organize Yourself*

The first student handout asks questions of your students to increase their awareness of their present organizing habits. Although the student worksheets assist in determining concrete solutions, these six questions will elicit a range of alternatives never before considered by your students. Because this is a brainstorming handout, all student input is considered valid, and is not judged or disputed. To keep the discussion on topic and spontaneous, write key words from the students' suggestions on the board. Conclude the discussion by showing similarities and differences in the students' responses.

Handout: *5 Ways to Organize Your Study Time*

The second student handout requires more instruction from you than discussion by your students. In addition to discussing the calendar samples for schoolwork, you may want to share samples of calendar use to plan students' social time or helping time at home. This handout stresses organizing to study for tests. Using the *wh* question cues (*who, what, where, when, why* and *how*) will give your students a way to remember how to organize their study time.

9

Worksheet: *Getting Organized to Study*

This worksheet is designed to help your students identify concrete behaviors regarding:

What their study habits <u>are</u> now, how their study habits could <u>improve</u>, and what specific behaviors they can <u>change</u> now.

This worksheet can be completed individually by each student, and discussed later in a group or privately with you.   If students have difficulty determining ways to change that are realistic and practical, ask questions to help them determine changes, such as:

If you study best at night, but you like to watch TV, too, can you use your calendar to plan to do both?

If no one at home can quiz you on your vocabulary definitions, is there someone who would help you over the phone or right after school?

Worksheet: *Planning Your Study Time to Take a Test*

This second worksheet gives your students practice plotting study time on a calendar.   If your students have difficulty doing the assignment independently, discuss items 1-6 and have them plot each day according to the questions:

What should you study?

When should you study? (day and time)

Who should you study with?

Where should you study?

How will you study?

Getting Organized to Study   Name _____

How well do you know yourself?   Think about your study habits as you answer these questions.

1. When do I study now?   After dinner
   When would I study best?   Right after school
   Here's what I can change: Start studying right after school

2. How do I study now?   While I watch TV
   How would I study best?   In a quiet place
   Here's what I can change: Study away from noise or TV

3. Where do I study now?   In the living room
   Where would I study best?   In my bedroom
   Here's what I can change: Study in my bedroom

4. What subjects are easy for me?   Math and P.E.
   What subjects are hardest?   History and English
   Here's what I can do to make my hardest subject easier:
   Reread the text before I do my homework

5. Who helps me study now?   Nobody
   Who would help me the most with my studying?   My brother
   Here's what I can change: Ask my brother to help me

6. How much time do I spend studying now?   1 hour per night
   How much study time would be best?   2 hours per night
   Here's what I can change: Spend more time studying

7. Do I use a calendar to plan my study time?   No
   Here's what I can change: Use a calendar to plan my studying

8. Do I ask for help when I need it?   Sometimes
   Here's what I can change: Ask for help whenever I need it

WORKSHEET   16   Copyright 1987 LinguiSystems, Inc.

Planning Your Study Time to Take a Test   Name _____

Here's a study problem for you to solve.   First, read the information.   Then, plan your study time on the calendar.   Last, list three things that would help you study better.   Think about things to have handy while you study, such as materials, snacks, and other books.

A. Problem

1. Today is Monday, April 2.

2. Your English teacher says you'll have a test on Friday, April 6.

3. The test will be on chapters 4 through 8 in your grammar book.

4. Chapters 4 through 8 are about nouns, verbs, adjectives, and adverbs.

5. You have trouble understanding the difference between adjectives and adverbs in chapter 5.

6. Fill in the study calendar below.   Remember to include:
    what to study each day
    when to study each day
    who to study with

Monday	Tuesday	Wednesday	Thursday	Friday
2	3	4	5	6
6:30 - 7:30 Study ch. 4 - 5 alone.	6:30 - 7:30 Study ch. 5 - 6 alone.	6:30 - 7:30 Study ch. 7 - 8 alone.	6:30 -7:30 Study ch. 4 - 8 alone.	2:00 grammar test
	7:30 - 8:00 Have Dad quiz me on adj. and adv.		7:30 - 8:30 Have Dad quiz me on all ch.	

B. Things that would help me study better:

1. glass of lemonade

2. chair cushion

3. bedroom door closed

WORKSHEET   17   Copyright 1987 LinguiSystems, Inc.

10

Worksheet: *Planning Your Homework Time to Write a Report*

This worksheet is another assignment to practice plotting homework time. Your students may need help with the definitions of "rough draft" and "final report." They may also need to know that reading the entire book about whales is not necessary if the book is long and detailed. You might also suggest that they use a reference book (encyclopedia, "All About..." series, etc.) to read about whales.

Planning Your Homework Time to Write a Report   Name _____

Writing a report can be easy if you plan your time. Read the information below. Then, plan your homework time. Last, list three things that would make your report writing easier.

A. Problem

1. Today is Monday, January 15.

2. You have a science report due on Friday, January 19.

3. Your science report is about whales.

4. The report must be two pages long.

5. You decide to use a book about whales from the library.

6. Your teacher wants you to write a rough draft first. The rough draft is due on Wednesday, January 17.

7. Fill in the calendar below. Remember to include:

   a trip to the library
   reading a part of the book about whales
   writing a rough draft
   getting the rough draft back from your teacher
   writing the final report

Monday	Tuesday	Wednesday	Thursday	Friday
2	3	4	5	6
After school – go to library – get whale book. 6:30 – 7:30 Read book about whales.	6:30 – 7:30 Write rough draft of whale rep't.	2:45 rough draft due – science rep't 6:30 – 7:30 Review whale book	2:45 get rough draft back 6:30 – 7:30 Write final whale rep't.	2:45 science report due

B. Things that would help me write my report:

1. dictionary _____

2. grammar book for punctuation rules _____

3. can of 7-Up _____

WORKSHEEET   18   Copyright © 1987 LinguiSystems, Inc.

6 Ways to Organize Yourself

Name _____

Organizing yourself helps you to do more work in less time.   Think about these six questions, and talk about your answers in class.   Find out how organized you are!

1   Find out <u>when</u> you do your best work.   Ask yourself, *When do I learn the best?*

   As soon as I come home from school?

   After a snack?

   After some free time?

   In the morning?

   In the evening?

2   Find out <u>how</u> you learn most easily.   Ask yourself, *How do I learn best?*

   When I study alone?

   When I rewrite my notes?

   When I study with someone?

   When I read or say things out loud?

   When someone else checks my work?

3   Find out <u>where</u> you study best.   Ask yourself, *Where is the best place for me to study?*

   In my room?

   In the den?

   At the kitchen table?

   In study hall?

   Away from the TV?

   Away from people?

4   Find out <u>why</u> you have different study habits for different subjects. Ask yourself, *Why do I study subjects differently?*

       Do I need to practice spelling words out loud?

       Do I need someone else to help me with math?

       Do I need to take notes when I read for history class?

       Do I need to underline the directions for science?

5   Find out <u>what</u> you study best. Ask yourself, *What subjects are easiest and hardest for me?*

       Math?

       English?

       Science?

       History?

6   Find out <u>who</u> can help you. Ask yourself, *Who can help me with my work at school?*

       Certain teachers?

       My counselor?

       Another student?

Now ask yourself, *Who can help me with my schoolwork at home?*

       My parents?

       My sister or brother?

       A neighbor?

       A friend?

5 Ways to Organize Your Study Time   Name _____

Do you spend study time watching TV or listening to music instead of studying?   Do you have trouble knowing what to study?   Here are five questions to ask yourself and talk about.   After you have talked about them, you'll be on your way to better study habits!

7   Find out <u>how</u> <u>long</u> your homework will take.   Ask yourself, *How much time will this work take me?*

   15 minutes?

   30 minutes?

   One hour?

   Many hours?

Decide how long your homework will take for each subject.   Then, use a monthly calendar to help you plan your time.   Suppose today is Monday, December 2. Below is the homework you have, the time you need to finish it, and the way you'll study.

   English — read Chapter 1 in *Tom Sawyer* — 30 minutes — alone

   Math — do problems 50-100, pages 34-35 — 20 minutes — Dad checks work

   Social Studies — study 10 geography definitions — 10 minutes — out loud

Here's how you could plan your homework on your calendar for tonight, Monday, December 2:

```
+-----------------------------------------------------------+
|        MONDAY                        | December 2 |
|  7:00-7:30  Read chapter 1 — Tom                          |
|             Sawyer — alone.                               |
|  7:30-7:50  Do Math pages 34-35,                          |
|             problems 50-100 — Dad                         |
|             checks.                                       |
|  7:50-8:00  Study 10 geography                            |
|             definitions — out loud.                       |
+-----------------------------------------------------------+
```

8   You can also use your calendar to plan the time to study for tests.   Ask yourself, *How much time do I need to study for my next test?*

   One hour?

   Two hours?

   Many hours?

9   Now ask yourself, *What are the best ways to study for the test?*

By myself, out loud?

By myself first, with Mom's help later?

With a friend?

By rewriting my notes?

By studying the hardest parts the longest and most often?

Let's try doing a study calendar.   Today is Monday, October 5.   Your teacher says you'll have a science test in one week, on October 12.   The test will be on the first two chapters in your book.   Write the science test on your calendar for October 12.   Then, plan your study time on your calendar, too.   Your study plan might look like this one.

Sunday	Monday	Tuesday	Wednesday	Thursday	Friday	Saturday
4	5 7:00-8:00 Reread Ch. 1 in Science.	6 7:00-7:30 Review Ch. 1 in Science. 7:30-8:00 Have Mom quiz me.	7 7:00-8:00 Reread Ch. 2 in Science.	8 7:00-7:30 Review Ch. 2 in Science. 7:30-8:00 Have Dad quiz me.	9 4:00-5:00 Dave and I quiz each other on Ch. 1-2 in Science.	10 15 minutes Tell Dad about Science Ch. 1-2.
11 2:00-3:00 Review science Ch. 1-2.	12 9:00 Science test.	13	14	15	16	17

Do you think this study plan gives you enough study time?   Will you still have time to study for other subjects?   Will you have free time, too?   By doing this study plan, you will know:

what to study

when to study

where to study

who to study with

how to study

how long to study

10   When you finish an assignment, cross it off your calendar.   If you didn't finish all your homework, add it to the next day.

11   Write on your calendar in pencil.   That way, changes are easy to erase!

15

Getting Organized to Study

Name _____

How well do you know yourself?   Think about your study habits as you answer these questions.

1. When do I study now? _____

   When would I study best? _____

   Here's what I can change: _____

2. How do I study now? _____

   How would I study best? _____

   Here's what I can change: _____

3. Where do I study now? _____

   Where would I study best? _____

   Here's what I can change: _____

4. What subjects are easy for me? _____

   What subjects are hardest? _____

   Here's what I can do to make my hardest subject easier:

   _____

5. Who helps me study now? _____

   Who would help me the most with my studying? _____

   Here's what I can change: _____

6. How much time do I spend studying now? _____

   How much study time would be best? _____

   Here's what I can change: _____

7. Do I use a calendar to plan my study time? _____

   Here's what I can change: _____

8. Do I ask for help when I need it? _____

   Here's what I can change: _____

Planning Your Study Time to Take a Test

Name _____

Here's a study problem for you to solve. First, read the information. Then, plan your study time on the calendar. Last, list three things that would help you study better. Think about things to have handy while you study, such as materials, snacks, and other books.

A. Problem

1. Today is Monday, April 2.

2. Your English teacher says you'll have a test on Friday, April 6.

3. The test will be on chapters 4 through 8 in your grammar book.

4. Chapters 4 through 8 are about nouns, verbs, adjectives, and adverbs.

5. You have trouble understanding the difference between adjectives and adverbs in chapter 5.

6. Fill in the study calendar below. Remember to include:

   what to study each day

   when to study each day

   who to study with

Monday	Tuesday	Wednesday	Thursday	Friday
2	3	4	5	6 *2:00 grammar test*

B. Things that would help me study better:

1. _____

2. _____

3. _____

Planning Your Homework Time
to Write a Report

Name _____

Writing a report can be easy if you plan your time.   Read the information below.   Then, plan your homework time.   Last, list three things that would make your report writing easier.

A.   Problem

1.   Today is Monday, January 15.

2.   You have a science report due on Friday, January 19.

3.   Your science report is about whales.

4.   The report must be two pages long.

5.   You decide to use a book about whales from the library.

6.   Your teacher wants you to write a rough draft first.   The rough draft is due on Wednesday, January 17.

7.   Fill in the calendar below.   Remember to include:

a trip to the library

reading a part of the book about whales

writing a rough draft

getting the rough draft back from your teacher

writing the final report

Monday	Tuesday	Wednesday	Thursday	Friday
2	3	4	5	6
				2:45 science report due

B.   Things that would help me write my report:

1.   _____

2.   _____

3.   _____

ORGANIZING YOUR MATERIALS

Not knowing how to organize books, notebooks, folders, worksheets, and an assignment book can cause as much confusion for students as not knowing how to organize study time. This section, Organizing Your Materials, is designed to help your students coordinate their school materials so that they don't forget to take home assignments and all the materials necessary to do the assignments.

To begin this unit, help your students recognize areas of needed improvement in organizing their materials. Ask them to

```
1 handout (pages 21-22)
2 worksheets (pages 23-24)
```

identify at least one organizational jumble they each have. Some responses might include:

My locker's a mess!

I never have all my homework done.

I forget my books at school.

I can't keep track of all my homework.

Handout: *7 Ways to Organize Your Materials*

This handout emphasizes seven concrete suggestions the students can implement immediately:

using an assignment book

using a notebook to take notes

coding notebooks, textbooks, and workbooks

filing returned papers

using a backpack or bookbag

having I.D. information on all important materials

organizing a locker

If you or your students can think of other ways to organize their materials, add them to the handout.

Worksheet: *Subjects, Materials, and Codes*

This worksheet gives your students a sorting task for learning the terminology of classroom subjects and materials, and for matching subject names with materials and codes. Suggest to your students that they progress down each column to accomplish this sorting task rather than choosing items at random. Students can check each other's work when the worksheet is completed.

Subjects, Materials, and Codes   Name _____

Before you can organize your materials, you need to know the names of many subjects and materials. You also need to think of codes to use. Sort the materials, subjects, and codes from the box into the correct columns.

English	triangle	notebook paper
math	grammar	green
biology	manual	folder
textbook	Spanish	history
star	yellow	ball
flag	health	workbook
science	blue	red
social studies	unicorn	geometry
assignment book	geography	notebook

SUBJECTS	MATERIALS	CODES
English	textbook	star
math	assignment book	flag
biology	manual	triangle
science	notebook paper	yellow
social studies	folder	blue
grammar	workbook	unicorn
Spanish	notebook	green
health		ball
geography		red
history		
geometry		

WORKSHEET   23   Copyright © 1987 LinguiSystems, Inc.

Worksheet: *Organizing Your Materials*

The second worksheet is designed to have your students practice more organizing through sorting. They also have the opportunity to determine a coding system.

Organizing Your Materials   Name _____

Help! These things need to be organized. Look carefully at each item in the box below. Each item tells you two things — the subject and type of material. Sort each subject under SUBJECTS and each book or folder under MATERIALS. Decide on a code for each subject and write it under CODES. The first one is done for you. Thanks for getting organized!

English textbook	science manual	social studies notebook
English workbook	social studies folder	science notebook
math textbook	English folder	history notebook
social studies textbook	math folder	math notebook
science folder	science textbook	history textbook

SUBJECTS	MATERIALS	CODES
English	English textbook	square
English	English workbook	square
English	English folder	square
math	math textbook	triangle
math	math folder	triangle
math	math notebook	triangle
social studies	social studies textbook	flag
social studies	social studies folder	flag
social studies	social studies notebook	flag
science	science folder	star
science	science manual	star
science	science textbook	star
science	science notebook	star
history	history notebook	apple
history	history textbook	apple

WORKSHEET   24   Copyright © 1987 LinguiSystems, Inc.

---

7 Ways to Organize Your Materials

Name _____

Have you ever left your homework at school? Have you ever lost a book? Well, keep reading! You'll find 7 helpful ways to organize your materials...so you don't forget!

12   Do you use an assignment notebook?   It's great for:

    writing down each homework assignment

    remembering which books to take home

    remembering to do all your homework

13   Do you use a notebook for your class notes?   Here are some tips:

    Use a different notebook for each subject.   Then your notes won't get mixed up.

    Put the date on each page.   Then you'll know when you took your notes.

    Use a three-ring binder with tab dividers for different subjects.   Then all your notes for all your subjects will be in one place.

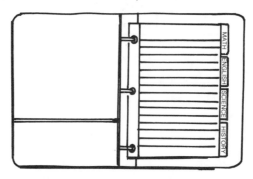

14   Do you code your notebooks, textbooks, and workbooks?   A color or design code will help you find all your books in your locker.   Then you won't forget to take anything home!   Here's how to use a code:

    Choose a color or special design for each subject.   Use one color or design on each notebook, textbook, and workbook for that subject.   Then, all your books for English will look the same, all your books for math will look the same, etc.

    If you choose a special design for each subject, cover your textbook with brown grocery bag paper.   Draw the design for that subject on the cover.   Also, write the subject name on the brown cover, such as ENGLISH.   Draw the same design on that subject's notebook and workbook and label them, too.

    If you choose a color for each subject, cover your textbook and workbook with colored paper.   Make your notebook the same color, too.   If you don't have colored paper, use brown grocery bag paper.   Then, use markers to give you the color you chose.

    Be sure to label each book with the subject name.

    If you use a three-ring binder, color or design-code the tab dividers to match your textbook and workbook for each subject.

15   Do you keep your papers your teachers return to you?   These papers can really help you.

     They can help you review for tests.

     They can help you write reports.

     Put them in subject folders that are coded the same as your other books.

     File the papers by date.

16   How do you carry your books to school?

     If you use a backpack or bookbag, clean it out every day.   That way, you won't lose your books or your homework.

     If you don't use a backpack, make sure loose papers are in your notebooks before you go outside.   Books are heavy enough without chasing after papers in the wind!

17   Do you have identifying information on your books?

     Label your books, notebooks, workbooks, assignment notebook, folders, and your backpack with:

        your name

        the name of the book

        the name of the class

        the period you have the class

        the name of the teacher

        the room where the class meets

18   Can you find things in your locker?   The codes on your books will help.   Here are some other tips.

     Keep your locker as neat as possible by throwing junk away each day.

     If you share a locker, decide which part is yours.   Then you can keep all your books and materials together.

     Use grocery bags, plastic bags, or small cartons to organize your part of a shared locker.   Loose papers, pens, books, and folders can turn your locker into a jumbled mess!

Subjects, Materials, and Codes

Name _____

Before you can organize your materials, you need to know the names of many subjects and materials. You also need to think of codes to use. Sort the materials, subjects, and codes from the box into the correct columns.

English	triangle	notebook paper
math	grammar	green
biology	manual	folder
textbook	Spanish	history
star	yellow	ball
flag	health	workbook
science	blue	red
social studies	unicorn	geometry
assignment book	geography	notebook

SUBJECTS   MATERIALS   CODES

_____   _____   _____

_____   _____   _____

_____   _____   _____

_____   _____   _____

_____   _____   _____

_____   _____   _____

_____   _____   _____

_____   _____

_____

Organizing Your Materials

Help! These things need to be organized. Look carefully at each item in the box below. Each item tells you two things — the subject and type of material. Sort each subject under SUBJECTS and each book or folder under MATERIALS. Decide on a code for each subject and write it under CODES. The first one is done for you. Thanks for getting organized!

English textbook	science manual	social studies notebook
English workbook	social studies folder	science notebook
math textbook	English folder	history notebook
social studies textbook	math folder	math notebook
science folder	science textbook	history textbook

SUBJECTS	MATERIALS	CODES
English	*English textbook*	*square*

ORGANIZING YOUR WORK AREA AT HOME

Where do your students study at home? Do they organize their work area? Do they have a special work place?

Even if they share their workspace with other family members, they will be more organized if they have one special spot for studying. Have your students list and discuss reasons to have an organized work area, such as:

> easy availability for studying
>
> knowing ahead of time where materials are located
>
> never having to look for lost materials
>
> allowing for adequate lighting and proper ventilation

> 1 handout (pages 26-27)
> 1 worksheet (page 28)

Maintaining a special spot for studying becomes much easier when your students establish a daily routine and make daily checks on their materials. Soon, the routine will be so common, they'll assume they've always been this organized at home!

Handout: *6 Ways to Get Organized at Home*

This two-page handout will help your students generate conversation for immediate problem-solving about their organization at home. You may want to emphasize the importance of establishing a routine at home, just like they have at school. Also, encourage your students to avoid studying in a place or chair that is too comfortable, such as a bed or a soft chair. They may get too sleepy to concentrate well.

Worksheet: *Let's Get Organized at Home*

This short chapter concludes with a worksheet that gives your students a chance to record the books and supplies they need to be organized every night at home. Have your students work on these independently. Then, checking against the list in the handout, have your students add the things they may have forgotten.

Let's Get Organized at Home   Name _____

Let's list all your necessary books and study supplies on this form. Can you think of some supplies you like or need that are special to you? List those, too!

Things I Need When I Study	Dates I Checked My Materials							
MATERIALS								
pencil								
pencil sharpener								
eraser								
pen								
paper								
tape								
glue								
scissors								
paper clips								
staples								
stapler								
index cards								
highlighter								
felt-tip markers								
ruler								
globe or map								
bookmark								
BOOKS								
assignment book								
dictionary								
workbooks								
textbooks								
notebooks								
subject folders								
OTHER								
clock								
snack								
glass of pop								
lamp								
eye glasses								
SPECIAL MATERIALS I LIKE OR NEED								
bright lamp								
box of raisins								
thesaurus								
chair cushion								

WORKSHEET   28   Copyright© 1987 LinguiSystems, Inc.

6 Ways to Get Organized at Home

Name _____

Getting organized to do your work at home is important, too. Talk about these 6 things you can do to get going on some good organizing at home!

19   Are there some good places for you to study at home?   Your list might include:

your room	at your desk
the kitchen	at the kitchen table
the den	at the dining room table

20   What books do you need each night?   Your list might include:

assignment book

textbooks

folders

notebooks

workbooks

21   What materials do you need <u>every</u> <u>time</u> you do homework?   Your list might include:

pencil	lamp	eyeglasses
pen	pencil sharpener	snack
eraser	clock	glass of water, juice,
paper	paper clips	or other beverage

22   What materials do you need often?   These materials should be near your work place:

dictionary	index cards	bookmark
highlighter	tape	globe or maps
scissors	glue	stapler
ruler	felt-tip markers	staples

23 Do you check to make sure you have everything you need before you begin you homework?   If you do, you'll avoid wasted time and too many interruptions.   Your checklist might look like this:

Things I Need When I Study	Dates I Checked My Materials									
MATERIALS										
pencil										
pencil sharpener										
eraser										
pen										
paper										
tape										
glue										
scissors										
paper clips										
stapler										
index cards										
highlighter										
felt-tip markers										
ruler										
globe or maps										
staples										
book mark										
BOOKS										
assignment book										
dictionary										
work books										
text books										
note books										
subject folders										
OTHER										
clock										
snack										
glass of water, etc.										
lamp										
eyeglasses										

24 Do you check your supplies often?   That way, you won't run out of paper when you have a report to write!

27

Let's Get Organized at Home

Name _____

Let's list all your necessary books and study supplies on this form. Can you think of some supplies you like or need that are special to you? List those, too!

Things I Need When I Study	Dates I Checked My Materials									
MATERIALS										
BOOKS										
OTHER										
SPECIAL MATERIALS I LIKE OR NEED										

USING AN ASSIGNMENT BOOK

Remembering what homework to do and the books needed to do it are two of the toughest memory tasks for students of all ages. The answer? Make remembering a writing task rather than a memory task. How? With the you-can't-get-along-in-school-without-one assignment book! This mighty little book or tablet can be the key to homework success. No forgotten assignments,

> 1 handout (page 31-34)
> 3 worksheets (pages 35-37)

no frantic phone calls to friends, no books left in their lockers...just total organization of homework and studying!

Handout: *10 Tips about Your Assignment Book*

This student handout emphasizes the *who, what, when, where, why,* and *how* of keeping an assignment book. It shows your students how and what to write for each subject, how to prioritize their homework each night, how to record the work they've already done, and how to prepare for the next day. It may take your students quite a while to understand and use their assignment books well, so review the handout after your students complete each worksheet.

Worksheet: *Your Assignment Book at Work*

The first worksheet gives your students practice in writing their actual homework assignments, and prioritizing their work and time. If your students find this a particularly difficult worksheet, assign fabricated homework for four subjects and include an item for Other Notes. Try to review your students' work immediately after they've finished.

Your Assignment Book at Work   Name _____

Now's the time to practice what you've learned. Write your homework for one day on this worksheet. Be sure to include:

  subjects
  chapter numbers
  number to do
  what to do
  order to do your homework

Date: **March 17, 1987**	
Order	Subject
2.	Math — Do pgs. 41-43, all problems in
	textbook. Have Dad check.
3.	Science — Read chapter 22, answer
	questions at end of chapter
	with Mom
1.	English — Test tomorrow on commas,
	periods, semicolons. Study
	textbook pgs. 156-210 with Ted.
Other Notes:	Bring 2 sharp pencils for English test.

1. What are some important words you wrote about the way you'll do each assignment?
   Have Dad check; with Mom; with Ted

2. How long will it take you to do each assignment? **1 hour for English;**
   ½ hour for math; ½ hour for science.

3. Why did you order the assignments in the way you did? **English test**
   tomorrow is most important.   Math is harder for me than science.

WORKSHEET   35   Copyright© 1987 LinguiSystems, Inc.

Worksheet: *What's Wrong Here?*

The second worksheet gives your students a chance to identify and correct mistakes. Again, feel free to do this worksheet along with your students, or assign it as independent work. You may also choose to indicate the errors to your students and have them make the corrections.

What's Wrong Here?   Name _____

Here's your chance to catch some mistakes! This page shows an assignment page. The student has finished her science and English assignments. Can you find and correct all mistakes and missing information on the page? List the mistakes you found at the bottom of your paper, and congratulations on catching all of them!

⊙ What date?
Math: p.62 What book? What problems?
What order?
Science: Study What?

English: ex. A & B, on note-
⊙ book paper. From what book?

History: Test Friday
What on?

Social Studies. None

⊙

Mistakes

1. date   5. English: what book?
2. order of homework   6. history: what is test on?
3. math: what book, problems 7. social studies: no homework
4. science: study what?

WORKSHEET   36   Copyright© 1987 LinguiSystems, Inc.

Worksheet: *Assignment Book Swap*

This last worksheet is meant to be done between at least two students. This worksheet encourages good-natured criticism of another's assignments for one day. You may chose to have the students critique a bonafide assignment page, or you can fabricate a day of assignments. The comments for suggestions and what was done well are meant to have your students be creative in their problem solving for the other person.

Assignment Book Swap   Name _____

Now, let's check to see how others are doing. Trade your assignment book with another student. Use the questions below to check your partner's assignment book. Your teacher will help you with this review if you need it.

Assignment Book Review

Student Owning Assignment Pad: __Joan__

Reviewer: __Sally__

		Yes	No
1.	Are the day and date at the top?	✔	
2.	Does each subject have enough room next to it to write the assignment?	✔	
3.	Is there enough space at the bottom of the page to write other notes?	✔	
4.	Is "none" written if there was no homework in a subject?		✔
5.	Did the student number the homework in order from hardest to easiest?		✔
6.	Did the student check off assignments that were finished?	✔	

Add your comments about what the student did well on his assignment page. Make a suggestion for improvement, too.

7. You did these well: __You dated your work and left enough room to write each__
__assignment. You checked off assignments you finished.__

_____

8. Suggestion: __Write "none" if you have no homework. Write the order in which__
__you'll do each assignment.__

_____

WORKSHEET   37   Copyright© 1987 LinguiSystems, Inc.

Assignment books are the best books around!   They help you remember what homework to do and which books to bring home.   They also help you remember other things you need to do.   Read on to discover the assignment book!

25   Find out what an assignment book looks like.   You can choose one of these:

　　　a small 8'' x 5'' notebook with about 200 pages of lined paper, enough for every day of the school year; or

　　　a preprinted assignment book that has a page printed for every day of the year; or

　　　a tablet of 200 sheets of blank paper.

26   If you use a preprinted assignment book, write in the subjects you have on every page from Mondays through Fridays.

27   If you use a plain notebook or tablet, write each day, date, and subject on each page.   Each page will look something like this:

Monday, November 7, 1987

Math

History

Science

English

Social Studies

Other notes

28   Save a small space at the bottom of each page for Other Notes. Use this space to remind yourself of other things you need to do.

29   The column on the far left will give you space to number the assignments from first-to-do to last. It will also give you a way to check off each assignment as you finish it.

30   How should you use your assignment book at school?

Open your assignment book as soon as you get to class.

Put it on your desk or on the floor near your seat.

As soon as your teacher says you'll have homework, get a pencil and your assignment book.

31   Writing the correct information in your assignment book is as important as doing the homework!

Write all the pages of the homework. Write any other important words, like ''read,'' ''outline,'' ''memorize,'' ''answer questions 1-8,'' etc.

If you don't have any homework in a class, write ''none.''

At the end of each class, check to make sure you have all the information you need to do your homework.

32   Keep your assignment book handy. If your assignment book is with you all day, every day, you'll remember to take it home. Before you leave school, check your assignment book to see which books you'll need to take home. Also, check Other Notes to see if you have any special plans after school.

33   Having your assignment book at home is the 'oomph' you may need to get your homework started!

Open your assignment book to the page for the day.

Review your homework assignments. Which one is the hardest? Which one is the easiest? Number the assignments in the order you decide to do them. A good rule is to begin with the hardest.

Make sure you have all the materials you need to do your homework.

34   After you finish each assignment, check it off in your assignment book. Then, when you're done with all your homework:

check the Other Notes to make sure you've done everything;

gather your books together for the next morning; and

write the day, date, and subjects on the next page for the next day.

Now, you're all set for tomorrow! Good job!

32

Here's an example of a well-organized assignment book.   The student has written in the assignments and other good notes.   The student has also numbered how she will do the assignments.

O	Monday, November 2, 1987
1.	Math — p. 62 #'s 1-71. Ask about #63 tomorrow. Test on Friday, p. 46-71.
3.	History — Read ch. 3. Take notes to study from.
O 2	English — Paper due Nov. 18 on space travel. Use To Travel Through Space book. Read 6 pgs. each night till next Thursday.
	Science — none
O	Other notes — Bring $5 for yearbook pictures tomorrow.

33

Look at this example of another student's assignment book.   Can you find some ways to improve it?   The errors are shown for you.   Talk about ways to make it better.

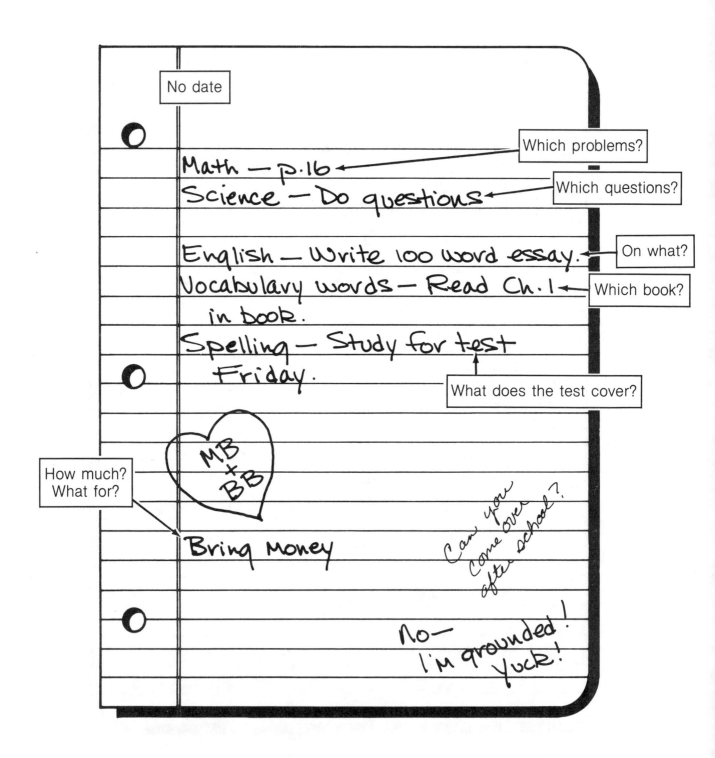

34

Your Assignment Book at Work   Name _____

Now's the time to practice what you've learned.   Write your homework for one day on this worksheet.   Be sure to include:

   subjects

   chapter numbers

   number to do

   what to do

   order to do your homework

Date:	
Order	Subject
Other Notes:	

1. What are some important words you wrote about the way you'll do each assignment?

   _____

2. How long will it take you to do each assignment? _____

   _____

3. Why did you order the assignments in the way you did? _____

   _____

What's Wrong Here?

Here's your chance to catch some mistakes!   This page shows an assignment page.   The student has finished her science and English assignments.   Can you find and correct all mistakes and missing information on the page?   List the mistakes you found at the bottom of your paper, and congratulations on catching all of them!

Math: p.62

Science: Study

English: ex. A & B, on notebook paper.

History: Test Friday

Social Studies:

Mistakes

1. _____

2. _____

3. _____

4. _____

5. _____

6. _____

7. _____

36

Assignment Book Swap

Name _____

Now, let's check to see how others are doing. Trade your assignment book with another student. Use the questions below to check your partner's assignment book. Your teacher will help you with this review if you need it.

Assignment Book Review

Student Owning Assignment Pad: _____

Reviewer: _____

	Yes	No
1. Are the day and date at the top?		
2. Does each subject have enough room next to it to write the assignment?		
3. Is there enough space at the bottom of the page to write other notes?		
4. Is "none" written if there was no homework in a subject?		
5. Did the student number the homework in order from hardest to easiest?		
6. Did the student check off assignments that were finished?		

Add your comments about what the student did well on his assignment page. Make a suggestion for improvement, too.

7. You did these well: _____

_____

_____

8. Suggestion: _____

_____

_____

SURVEYING

Surveying reading material is a skill your students are probably using already. They survey several books before picking just one or two from the library. They survey their favorite magazines at the drugstore before buying one. They also survey TV shows, by turning from one channel to another, before selecting the one to watch. You can en-

> 1 handout (page 41-42)
> 2 worksheets (pages 43-44)

courage further development of this skill by showing your students the specifics of what they're already doing.

Handout: *Surveying Your Reading Material*

The specifics of surveying are presented in this handout, which stresses surveying the outside <u>and</u> inside of a book or magazine. Begin by looking at the jacket or cover of the material. Note the:

title

author

author or article information

book review

pictures or photographs

What do these features tell your students about the book or magazine? Next, survey the inside of the reading material. Point out the:

copyright date

table of contents and chapter titles

introduction, foreword, or prologue

dedication

size of print

number of pages

use of graphics or artwork

Then, help your students understand the differences between fiction, non-fiction, and biographies or autobigraphies. Bring examples to talk about.

Worksheet: *A Survey of the Newspaper*

This first worksheet guides your students through the process of reviewing your local paper for determining what to read. Although newspapers are not likely to have introductions, appendices, or chapters, they will have:

    name of newspaper (title)
    headlines or section names (chapter titles)
    by-lines (authors)
    table of contents
    graphics and artwork
    articles (chapters)

Have your students each survey a page from your local newspaper.   When they are finished, have each of them tell you:

    who wrote one of the articles

    what the article might be about

    what is known from pictures

    where the article would be listed in the table of contents

    if the information is fact or opinion

To complete this worksheet, have each student decide whether the article is of interest to him.

Worksheet: *Doing Your Own Surveying*

The second worksheet is meant to guide your students through the process of surveying without your help.   Select books for your students to survey, and give them 20 to 30 minutes to complete the worksheet.   Discuss each student's worksheet with him, spending the most time on questions 3 and 4.   These questions require supposition on the student's part.

A Survey of the Newspaper   Name _____

Although a newspaper does not have a story like a book does, it can be just as much fun to read.   A newspaper has many articles and sections that have news, entertainment, and advertising.   Most newspapers have the following sections:

1   The main or first section contains articles about very important national, state, and local issues.   You might find an editorial here.   An editorial is an article written by the editor of your newspaper.   It states an opinion about something in the news.

2   The sports section has articles about sporting events from around the world and around your town.

3   The business section reports facts and features about industry and business in the U.S. and around the world.   You'll find the stock market report here.

4   The local section reports news about your community.   Obituaries (deaths) and births are reported here.

5   The entertainment section tells you news about TV shows, movies, plays, and music.   You might find the comic strips or crossword puzzle here.

6   The classified advertisement section is the place to look to find a job, buy a house, rent an apartment, buy a car, or to find just about anything else you want to buy or rent.   You might find the comic strips or crossword puzzle here, too.

Now that you see how a newspaper is put together, let's see what you can learn about the page your teacher gives you.   Answer the questions below.

1   What is the name of your newspaper?   __Chicago Tribune__

2   What section do you think your page is from?   __Sports__

3   What is the date of your paper?   __March 6, 1987__

4   What is a main headline on your page?   __Troubles at World Indoor Meet__

5   What is the main article about?   __U.S. track athletes don't have enough money to train and compete.__

6   Is there a picture that goes with the article?   If so, what does it tell you?
    __No__

7   Where might your page be listed in the Table of Contents?   __Front page__

8   Is the article fact or opinion?   __Fact__

9   Who wrote the article?   __Phil Hersh__

WORKSHEET   43   Copyright© 1987 LinguiSystems, Inc.

Doing Your Own Surveying   Name _____

Now, try surveying on your own.   Survey a book you have not read before, chosen by you or your teacher.   Then, fill in this worksheet with your answers.

1.   What is the title of the book?   What could the title mean?
     __The Red Badge of Courage__   __Someone got a badge for doing something brave.__

2.   What kind of reading is it?   Is it fiction, nonfiction, etc.?
     __Fiction__

3.   What is the author's name?   What do you know about the author?
     __Stephen Crane__   __He lived from 1871-1900.   He wrote many books.__

4.   What year was the book written?   Does the time the book was written tell you why the author wrote the book?   If so, how does it tell you?
     __1895__   __This book is about the Civil War.__   __Many people were still thinking about the Civil War when this book was written.__

5.   Does the book have a prologue, introduction, or foreword?   Does it tell you something interesting about the book?   If so, how?
     __The introduction reviews the author's background and the book's history.__

6.   How many pages are in the book?   __409__   Is the print size easy to read?   Why or why not?
     __The print is small, but it's not hard to read.__

7.   Does the book have any photographs, graphs, or drawings?   If so, describe one.
     __One drawing shows soldiers lying down, ready to fire guns.__

8.   What do you think of this book?
     __It tells a lot about bravery and war.   I'd like to read it.__

WORKSHEET   44   Copyright© 1987 LinguiSystems, Inc.

Surveying Your Reading Material   Name _____

Before you begin reading a book, what do you know about it?   Lots!   By surveying, or looking the book over, you can find out about the author, the story, the people in the book, and much more.   Surveying can help you know what to expect from the book.   Surveying can also help you review a book you have already read before.

35   Knowing these words about books can help you when you survey.   Use a textbook and see how its content compares to these words.

An **appendix** at the end of a book tells about other books or information related to the book.

An **author** is the person who wrote the book.

A **biography** is the true story of a person's life.

A **chapter** is a part or section of a book.

Fiction is a story the author makes up.

A **foreword** or **preface** is in the front of a book.   It is a note from the author telling you something special about the book.

A **graph**, **drawing**, or **photograph** tells you something in pictures rather than words.

An **introduction** at the beginning of the book gets you ready to read the book.   It introduces you to the people, places, and time of the story.

Nonfiction is a true story based on facts.

A **prologue** comes before a story.   The prologue is like a little story before the main one.   It tells something important that happened before the story began.

A **table of contents** tells you what is in the book and where to find it.

A **title** is the name of a book, chapter, or story.

36   Now that you've learned the words about surveying, let's see how they help us survey a book.   Ask yourself these questions and discuss them with your teacher.

What is the title?   What do you think the title means?

When was the book written?   The date may help you understand why the author wrote the book.

What kind of book is it?   Is it fiction or non-fiction?   Is it a biography?

What is the author's name?   Can you find information about the author on the book cover?   Does this information help you understand why the author wrote the book?

Is there a prologue, introduction, or foreword?   If so, what do these tell you about the book?

Is there a table of contents?   What does the table of contents tell you?

What do the titles of the chapters tell you about the book?

How many pages are there?

What is the size of the print?   Is it easy or hard to read?

Are there any pictures, graphs, or drawings in the book?   If so, does the artwork help you understand the story better?

What do you think of the book?   Does this look like a book you want to read?   Why or why not?

42

A Survey of the Newspaper

Name _____

Although a newspaper does not have a story like a book does, it can be just as much fun to read.   A newspaper has many articles and sections that have news, entertainment, and advertising.   Most newspapers have the following sections:

1.   The main or first section contains articles about very important national, state, and local issues.   You might find an editorial here.   An editorial is an article written by the editor of your newspaper.   It states an opinion about something in the news.

2.   The sports section has articles about sporting events from around the world and around your town.

3.   The business section reports facts and features about industry and business in the U.S. and around the world.   You'll find the stock market report here.

4.   The local section reports news about your community.   Obituaries (deaths) and births are reported here.

5.   The entertainment section tells you news about TV shows, movies, plays, and music.   You might find the comic strips or crossword puzzle here.

6.   The classified advertisement section is the place to look to find a job, buy a house, rent an apartment, buy a car, or to find just about anything else you want to buy or rent.   You might find the comic strips or crossword puzzle here, too.

Now that you see how a newspaper is put together, let's see what you can learn about the page your teacher gives you.   Answer the questions below.

1.   What is the name of your newspaper?   _____

2.   What section do you think your page is from?   _____

3.   What is the date of your paper?   _____

4.   What is a main headline on your page?   _____

5.   What is the main article about? _____

_____

6.   Is there a picture that goes with the article?   If so, what does it tell you?

_____

7.   Where might your page be listed in the Table of Contents?   _____

8.   Is the article fact or opinion?   _____

9.   Who wrote the article?   _____

Doing Your Own Surveying   Name _____

Now, try surveying on your own.   Survey a book you have not read before, chosen by you
or your teacher.   Then, fill in this worksheet with your answers.

1.   What is the title of the book?   What could the title mean?

_____

_____

2.   What kind of reading is it?   Is it fiction, nonfiction, etc.?

_____

3.   What is the author's name?   What do you know about the author?

_____

_____

4.   What year was the book written?   Does the time the book was written tell you why
the author wrote the book?   If so, how does it tell you?

_____

_____

5.   Does the book have a prologue, introduction, or foreword?   Does it tell you
something interesting about the book?   If so, how?

_____

6.   How many pages are in the book?   _____   Is the print size easy to read?   Why or
why not?

_____

7.   Does the book have any photographs, graphs, or drawings?   If so, describe one.

_____

8.   What do you think of this book?

_____

UNDERLINING OR HIGHLIGHTING

Learning to highlight or underline effectively is the study skill that makes the difference between effective and ineffective textbook reading. Underlining is also essential when reviewing class notes and reading directions on tests or worksheets. Although most students are not allowed to highlight their textbooks, they can be encouraged to highlight notes and newspaper or magazine articles. This chapter will show your students the important elements of underlining. Be pre-

> 3 handouts (pages 47-51)
> 2 worksheets (pages 52-53)

pared to cover this information slowly and with repeated practice. Few people know how to highlight to get the maximum benefit. You'll be sharing ways to achieve success in underlining with the following information.

Handout: *15 Ways to Underline or Highlight Your Reading*

This first handout stresses the importance of underlining to improve memory of what was read, to pick out the most important information to remember, to improve concentration, and to save time later when studying for a test. Discuss each point of effective underlining and supplement the examples with ones more relevant to your students.

Handouts: *Amelia Earhart* and *Fever*

The second and third handouts are two short passages which demonstrate effective underlining. See if your students can find the answers to the questions following each passage. As you read these aloud, stop along the way to discuss why certain words and phrases are underlined. Have your students determine whether any other important information has not been underlined. For additional examples, supplement these handouts with underlined or highlighted passages of your own.

Worksheets: *Underlining to Learn* and
              More Underlining to Learn

Both of these worksheets present short passages for your students to underline and questions for them to answer to evaluate the effectiveness of their underlining.

Again, feel free to supplement these worksheets with practice material of your own.   Some suggestions are:

passages from popular books

articles from popular magazines

free brochures from community businesses

advertising flyers enclosed in newspapers

catalogs

comic books

other pages of this book

recipes from cookbooks

Underlining to Learn   Name _____

Do you know which animal is the biggest in the world?   Underline the important information in the following paragraphs.   Check to make sure you've underlined all the information you need to answer the three questions.   Then, choose the best word to finish each question below.   Then, answer each question.

The Elephant

The elephant is the biggest land animal.   Its large nose is a long trunk that the elephant uses as a hand.   Elephants also have the biggest ears in the world.   Their tusks are large teeth.   An elephant's skin is one inch thick.

Elephants have been used in war, in circuses, at zoos, and as work animals.   Most elephants are peaceful animals.   However, their large size makes them dangerous when they are angry or frightened.   Scared elephants scream very loudly and flap their ears.   Trainers treat elephants kindly to get them to obey orders.   Well-trained elephants remember as many as thirty commands.   There seems to be some truth to the saying, "An elephant never forgets."

1.   __What__ is special about an elephant?   __An elephant is the biggest__
     Where / What
     __land animal__.

2.   __How__ have elephants been used?   __They have been used in circuses,__
     How / Who
     __at zoos, and as work animals__.

3.   __What__ do elephants do when they are scared?   __They scream and__
     When / What
     __flap their ears__.

WORKSHEET   52   Copyright © 1987 LinguiSystems, Inc.

More Underlining to Learn   Name _____

Is your house or apartment safe and secure?   Underline the paragraph to find the information to answer the questions.   Then, choose the best word to finish each question below.   Then, answer each question.

Home Security

A big worry for many homeowners and people who live in apartments is home security.   Home security means keeping your home safe from harmful people.   Police officers suggest putting deadbolt locks on all outside doors to keep your home safe from intruders.   The type of locks with tumblers and keys are most recommended.   It is wise to talk to children about how to answer the phone and the door when they are at home alone.   Also, keep important telephone numbers close to the phone.   For further information and tips about home security, call your local police department.

1.   __What__ is home security?   __Home security is keeping your home safe.__

2.   __Who__ knows about home security?   __Police officers__

3.   __Which__ type of locks are recommended?   __Locks with tumblers and keys__

4.   __What__ should children be taught to do?   __How to answer the phone and the__
     __door when they are at home alone__

5.   __What__ should you keep by the phone?   __Important phone numbers__

WORKSHEET   53   Copyright © 1987 LinguiSystems, Inc.

15 Ways to Underline or Highlight Your Reading

Name _____

Remembering what you read can be difficult.   Have you ever underlined or highlighted words with a colored marker?   Underlining or highlighting helps you pick out the most important information to remember.   Then, when it comes time to study for a test, you can save time by concentrating on the underlined or highlighted information.   You won't need to read all the material again when you underline!

Here's a list of helpful hints about how to underline or highlight what you read.

37   Read a whole paragraph first before underlining.

38   Go back to the beginning of the paragraph.   Now, you're ready to begin underlining.

39   Put a mark like a star or a check by pictures, graphs, and picture descriptions.   Your special marks will tell you to review these for important information.

⭐ There are many <u>castles</u> on the <u>Rhine River</u> in Germany.

40   Don't underline questions.   Sometimes the most important information is in the sentence that comes after the question.

Why did Columbus sail across the ocean?   He wanted to <u>find another way to get to the Far East</u>.

41   Try not to underline whole sentences.

President <u>Lincoln</u> tried to <u>listen to both sides</u>.

42   Usually, you will underline the first sentence in a paragraph.

Iron and steel are useful and cheap metals.   They are used to make hundreds of items.

Sometimes, the first sentence is not important.   In that case, underline the second sentence.

Much time passed.   Leaders of our country tried to solve the problem of slavery. They tried to end the arguing.   No one wanted a war.

43   Most of the time, you will underline the last sentence of a paragraph.

An insect is a small, six-legged animal.   There are about 800,000 kinds of insects.   Scientists think there are from one to ten million insects they haven't discovered yet.

If the last sentence is not important, underline the sentence before it.

People of the North believed slavery was wrong.   People of the South thought slavery was needed to keep the plantations running.   People from the West and East wanted to join the country.   These people had to decide whether to allow slavery or not.   Everyone didn't agree.

44   Underline proper nouns that name a person, place, thing, or idea.   A proper noun starts with a capital letter.

President Lincoln wanted to keep the Union together.

45   Underline words in italics, quotation marks, or bold print.

Lincoln believed that *all people should be free.*

People of the north were called "Yankees."

The **Declaration of Independence** was accepted on July 4, 1776.

46   Underline dates and numbers.

The Civil War began on April 12, 1861.

There were 529,332 people killed during the Civil War.

47   Underline long or strange words or phrases.   Look up the meanings of any words you don't know.   Write the words and definitions in your class notebook.

The White House is the official residence of the President of the United States.

48 Words like *for example* and abbreviations such as *e.g.* tell you that examples
follow. Examples usually do not need to be underlined.

<u>Many fruits</u> can be <u>cooked</u>. For example, strawberries and cherries can be baked
in pies.

49 Add notes in the margin to help you find the information you need to review.

The North and the South fought the Civil War over the idea of slavery. By the
end of the war, other issues had been fought over, too. All these issues revolved
around the issue that President Lincoln believed in so strongly:
<u>that all men are created equal</u>. ⟵————————— MAJOR
                                                              ISSUE

50 Use brackets or arrows to show a large amount of important information.

(Clean an open wound with soap and water. Cover the wound with a clean
  cloth. To stop bleeding, press hard on the wound. Change the bandage often.)

51 Look at the headings of a chapter or section. Use them, to help form questions that
will help you learn the most important information. Then find the answers to these
questions in the text and underline them. For example, a heading called *The Civil
War* can be turned into several questions to tell what the section is about. Use the
words *who*, *what*, *when*, *where*, *why*, or *how* to form your questions.

What was the Civil War?

When was the Civil War?

Where was the Civil War?

Who was in the Civil War?

Why was the Civil War fought?

How did the Civil War end?

Asking these questions tells us the information to look for as we read.

Amelia Earhart

Name _____

Here is a story with questions that will help you find the important information. The important information has been underlined, also, so that you can see an example. Read the story and the questions. See if the important information has been underlined so that you can answer the questions.

Amelia Earhart

Amelia Earhart was born in 1897 in Kansas. She was a nurse for wounded soldiers in World War I. Then, she went to a university and became a social worker. Her real interest was in airplanes. She saved her money to take flying lessons. In 1928, Amelia was the first woman passenger to go across the ocean in an airplane.

Amelia wrote a book about where she flew and her love of flying. She was the first woman to fly across the United States by herself. In 1937, she set out alone to go around the world. No one ever saw her or heard from her again. Amelia Earhart received the Distinguished Flying Cross in honor of her work with flight.

Who was Amelia Earhart?

What is Amelia Earhart known for?

When did Amelia Earhart do something important?

Where did Amelia Earhart do something important?

Why did Amelia Earhart do something important?

How did Amelia Earhart do something important?

Fever

Here is another article about health with the most important parts underlined.   See if you can find the information to answer the questions at the end of the article.

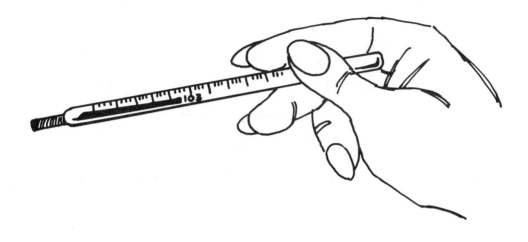

Fever

A *fever* is a body temperature that is higher than normal.   A normal temperature is 98.6°.   When a person has a fever, the body makes more heat than it gives off.   The body temperature can rise to 105° or more.   Fever is a sign, or symptom, of disease or illness.   A slight fever is often a sign of infection.   Other symptoms that go with a fever are thirst, a fast heartbeat, less energy, and general restlessness.   Scientists have found that a high fever can kill bacteria which cause some diseases.   A fever is one of nature's ways to heal the body.

What is a fever?

Why is a fever good to have?

Why do we get a fever?

How do we act when we have a fever?

51

Underlining to Learn   Name _____

Do you know which animal is the biggest in the world?   Underline the important information in the following paragraphs.   Check to make sure you've underlined all the information you need to answer the three questions.   Then, choose the best word to finish each question below.   Then, answer each question.

The Elephant

The elephant is the biggest land animal.   Its large nose is a long trunk that the elephant uses as a hand.   Elephants also have the biggest ears in the world.   Their tusks are large teeth.   An elephant's skin is one inch thick.

Elephants have been used in war, in circuses, at zoos, and as work animals.   Most elephants are peaceful animals.   However, their large size makes them dangerous when they are angry or frightened.   Scared elephants scream very loudly and flap their ears.   Trainers treat elephants kindly to get them to obey orders.   Well-trained elephants remember as many as thirty commands.   There seems to be some truth to the saying, "An elephant never forgets."

1. _____ is special about an elephant?   _____
   Where   What

_____

2. _____ have elephants been used?   _____
   How   Who

_____

3. _____ do elephants do when they are scared?   _____
   When   What

_____

More Underlining to Learn   Name _____

Is your house or apartment safe and secure?   Underline the paragraph to find the
information to answer the questions.   Then, choose the best word to finish each question
below.   Then, answer each question.

Home Security

A big worry for many homeowners and people who live in apartments

is home security.   Home security means keeping your home safe from

harmful people.   Police officers suggest putting deadbolt locks on all outside

doors to keep your home safe from intruders.   The type of locks with

tumblers and keys are most recommended.   It is wise to talk to children

about how to answer the phone and the door when they are at home alone.

Also, keep important telephone numbers close to the phone.   For further

information and tips about home security, call your local police department.

1. _____ is home security?   _____

2. _____ knows about home security?   _____

3. _____ type of locks are recommended?   _____

4. _____ should children be taught to do?   _____

   _____

5. _____ should you keep by the phone?   _____

SKIMMING

The concept of skimming may be unfamiliar to your students. Reading may be difficult for them, and comprehending material that has been passed over quickly may seem even more difficult. Therefore, your presentation of this material will be determined by your students' rate of learning and confidence in using the newly acquired skill. Although this skill may be somewhat tricky to teach, the previously learned skills of surveying and underlining have built a strong foundation for learning the skill of skimming.

> 2 handouts (pages 58-59)
> 5 worksheets (pages 60-64)

Handout: *8 Ways to Skim a Book*

The first handout of this unit emphasizes the 8 important elements of skimming as a way to <u>preview</u> and <u>review</u> reading material. As you present this handout, remind your students that the skills they learned for surveying and underlining are being applied to skimming.

Handout: *Skimming in Action*

The second handout shows your students how to skim by reading only the underlined material. The underlined material is the most important information in this passage. The most important information usually answers the *wh*-questions *who, what, when, where, why,* and *how.*

The five worksheets in this unit about skimming are designed to provide skimming practice for the student and also to provide a way of evaluating mastery of the skill by the student and you.

Worksheet: *Skimming and Underlining, Too*

This worksheet requires your students to underline only what they skim. Your students may be inclined to read the passage word for word. Encourage them to move their eyes quickly along each line and underline or highlight what they think looks important. Their skills with skimming will improve measurably with practice!

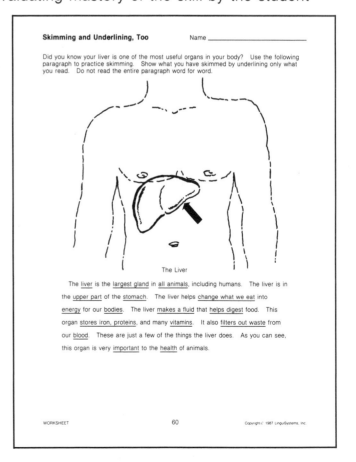

Worksheets: *How to Skim a Skeleton* and *Questions about* The Skeleton

Worksheets two and three are meant as practice for skimming and evaluation of the students' ability to skim. The comprehension questions contained in *Questions about the Skeleton* should be answered without the use of the passage. You may choose to restrict the amount of time your students have to skim the skeleton passage (2 minutes, perhaps) as a way of encouraging skimming rather than reading word for word.

How to Skim a Skeleton   Name _____

Skim this article. You may underline what you skim, if you choose. As soon as you have skimmed one time, turn your paper over. Then, answer the questions on the next page.

The Skeleton

The human skeleton is a wonderful building. It is the framework of your body. The skeleton gives you your shape. The skeleton also supports your tissues and protects your organs.

Your skeleton consists of all your bones, from the skull of your head to the tiny bones of your toes. Bones are hard in adults, but soft in babies. Bones are covered with a thin, strong skin. The spaces inside bones are filled with a fluid that helps carry blood. Learning about the skeleton reminds you to take good care of your bones.

WORKSHEET   61   Copyright© 1987 LinguiSystems, Inc

Questions about *The Skeleton*   Name _____

1. What is a skeleton? __The framework of our bodies_____

2. What are the two main functions of the skeleton? __Give us our shape;_____ __Support our tissues and protect our organs.__

3. How is an adult's bone different than a baby's bone? __An adult's bone is__ __hard. A baby's bone is soft.__

4. Bones are covered with __skin._____

5. Spaces inside our bones are filled with __fluid that helps carry blood.__

How well did you skim *The Skeleton*?

WORKSHEET   62   Copyright© 1987 LinguiSystems, Inc

56

Worksheets: *Warming Up to Skimming* and *Questions about* Thermometer or Thermostat?

Worksheets four and five should be presented in the same way as the worksheets for the skeleton passage. You should begin seeing improvement in your students' performance. You may wish to provide supplemental practice to your students if you are not satisfied with their mastery of skimming. Don't give up, though! With plenty of practice and ''warm fuzzies'' from you, your students will become champion skimmers!

Warming Up to Skimming Name _____

Here's another exercise to keep your skimming skills sharp. Skim these paragraphs once. You may choose to underline. Turn your paper over as soon as you are done. Then, answer the questions on the next page.

Thermometer or Thermostat?

What is the difference between a thermostat and a thermometer? Both are instruments and both deal with temperature. But that's where the likeness ends. These two instruments are very different in the ways they are used.

A thermometer is a measuring instrument. It is a sealed tube with a liquid inside and a numbered scale outside. A thermometer shows the temperature by the liquid that goes up or down as the temperature changes.

A thermostat is an automatic device. It works automatically by electricity. The thermostat *controls* the temperature instead of *showing* it. A thermostat actually changes the amount of gas or electricity supplied to a furnace.

Questions about *Thermometer or Thermostat?* Name _____

1. What two things are compared? __A thermometer and a thermostat__

2. How are these two items similar? __Both are instruments; both deal with temperature.__

3. Which one controls temperature? __Thermostat__

4. What does a thermometer do? __Shows the temperature__

5. Which holds a liquid that goes up and down? __Thermometer__

6. To change temperature, a thermostat controls the amount of __gas or electricity__ supplied to a furnace.

Bet your skimming skills are really hot, now!

8 Ways to Skim a Book

Have you ever skimmed a book?   To *skim* means to look something over quickly. Skimming gives you information about the main idea of your book.   When you skim, you don't read word for word.   Instead, you look it over quickly, noticing the most important information.   You skim before you underline.   Also, you can skim after you've underlined... then you skim only what you've underlined!

Here's how to skim as you read.   These hints are similar to the ones you learned in underlining.

52   Read the first sentence of each paragraph.   It usually has important information.

53   Notice proper names.   These begin with capital letters.   Proper names are important words to remember.   They tell you the name of a person, place, thing, or idea.

54   Pay attention to words in *italics*, "quotation marks," or **bold print**.   These special markings are used to show important words.

55   Notice dates and numbers.   They will tell you when and how many times something happened.

56   If you see a question mark, read on.   The most important information is usually found in the next sentence.

57   Stop and read long and unfamiliar words or phrases.   Look up the definitions in the dictionary.

58   Read the last sentence of each paragraph.   It usually has important information, too.

59   Remember, skimming just gives the main idea.   You will want to read and study the material more carefully at another time.

You can use skimming to look over your textbook chapters, library books, homework, or anything!   Then, when you're ready to study or read, you'll know what work needs to be done and how long it will take.   What a great way to help you plan your time!

Now, let's see some skimming in action.　Read the paragraph below.　The sentences are numbered for you.　Notice the underlined sections as you skim the paragraph.　Try not to read every word.

Jewelry

[1]Jewelry is a decoration or an ornament that people wear.　[2]Jewelry includes rings, bracelets, necklaces, and earrings.　[3]These pieces can be made of gold, silver, precious stone, wood, bone, seeds, shells, glass, and rocks.　[4]Some jewelry is very expensive.　[5]Other jewelry, called costume jewelry, costs much less.　[6]The difference in price depends on the amount of time and kind of materials that went into the making of the jewelry. [7]People have always worn jewelry to make themselves look more beautiful.

Here are some reasons the underlined parts are the most important parts to skim:

Sentence 1:　tells what jewelry is

Sentence 2:　tells what kind of jewelry there is

Sentence 3:　tells what jewelry is made of

Sentences 4 & 5:　tell how costly jewelry is

Sentence 6:　tells what makes jewelry costly

Sentence 7:　tells why people wear jewelry

Skimming and Underlining, Too

Name _____

Did you know your liver is one of the most useful organs in your body?   Use the following paragraph to practice skimming.   Show what you have skimmed by underlining only what you read.   Do not read the entire paragraph word for word.

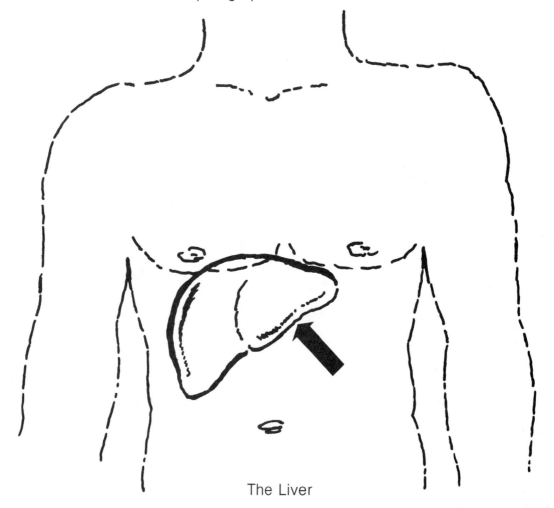

The Liver

The liver is the largest gland in all animals, including humans.   The liver is in the upper part of the stomach.   The liver helps change what we eat into energy for our bodies.   The liver makes a fluid that helps digest food.   This organ stores iron, proteins, and many vitamins.   It also filters out waste from our blood.   These are just a few of the things the liver does.   As you can see, this organ is very important to the health of animals.

How to Skim a Skeleton

Name _____

Skim this article.   You may underline what you skim, if you choose.   As soon as you have skimmed one time, turn your paper over.   Then, answer the questions on the next page.

The Skeleton

The human skeleton is a wonderful building.   It is the framework of your body.   The skeleton gives you your shape. The skeleton also supports your tissues and protects your organs.

Your skeleton consists of all your bones, from the skull of your head to the tiny bones of your toes.   Bones are hard in adults, but soft in babies.   Bones are covered with a thin, strong skin.   The spaces inside bones are filled with a fluid that helps carry blood.   Learning about the skeleton reminds you to take good care of your bones.

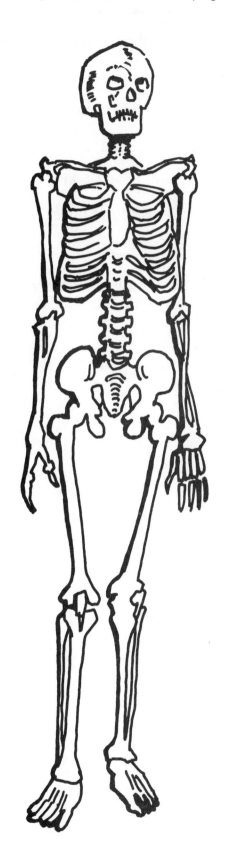

Questions about *The Skeleton*   Name _____

1.   What is a skeleton? _____

_____

2.   What are the two main functions of the skeleton? _____

_____

3.   How is an adult's bone different than a baby's bone? _____

_____

4.   Bones are covered with _____

5.   Spaces inside our bones are filled with _____

_____

How well did you skim *The Skeleton*?

Here's another exercise to keep your skimming skills sharp.   Skim these paragraphs once.   You may choose to underline.   Turn your paper over as soon as you are done.   Then, answer the questions on the next page.

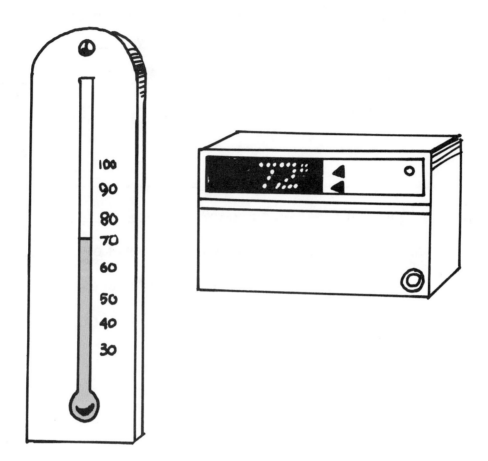

Thermometer or Thermostat?

What is the difference between a thermostat and a thermometer?   Both are instruments and both deal with temperature.   But that's where the likeness ends.   These two instruments are very different in the ways they are used.

A thermometer is a measuring instrument.   It is a sealed tube with a liquid inside and a numbered scale outside.   A thermometer shows the temperature by the liquid that goes up or down as the temperature changes.

A thermostat is an automatic device.   It works automatically by electricity. The thermostat *controls* the temperature instead of *showing* it.   A thermostat actually changes the amount of gas or electricity supplied to a furnace.

63

Questions about *Thermometer or Thermostat?*

Name _____

1. What two things are compared? _____

2. How are these two items similar? _____

    _____

3. Which one controls temperature? _____

4. What does a thermometer do? _____

    _____

    _____

5. Which holds a liquid that goes up and down? _____

6. To change temperature, a thermostat controls the amount of _____

    _____ supplied to a furnace.

Bet your skimming skills are really hot, now!

OUTLINING

Do you remember the endless practice you had to do to learn outlining? Do you remember how much you had to practice and how grateful you were later for knowing how to make good outlines? Well, we don't guarantee your students will love outlining, but we do know they can learn the skill of informal outlining and use it to improve their studying!

Like other skills this book teaches, the skill of outlining will help your students organize and remember what they hear or read. The best way we know to teach outlining, especially to slower learners, is to stress a) the outline title, b) the main topics, c) the subtopics, and d) the supporting details. Teaching additional sub-

```
3 handouts (pages 68-72)
3 worksheets (pages 73-75)
```

divisions of outlining may be reserved for advanced junior and senior high school students. Also, we have found the use of Roman numerals in outlines to be confusing to our language- and learning-disabled students. Use an alphanumeric system, instead. Later, when your students grasp the pattern of an outline, you may wish to introduce the use of Roman numerals.

Handout: *4 Parts to an Outline*

This first handout teaches the main essentials of a good outline. It stresses using words and phrases rather than full sentences in the outline, and parallels the "building" of an outline to the building of a house. Use whatever analogies work with your students to teach that they should always begin outlining with the most important information and end with the least important information.

Handouts: *Horsing Around with Outlining, Outline of* Horses, and *Outline of* Seasons of the Year

The second, third, and fourth handouts present short passages and illustrate how they can be outlined. As your students read each passage aloud with you, have them underline what they think is the best information to include in the outline. Then, they can compare what they thought should go in the outline to what was included in the handouts as a guide.

Finally, after much practice with you on outlining, it is time for your students to try outlining on their own. Worksheets one, two, and three provide a systematic approach to outlining independently.

Worksheets: *Outlining For Your Health* and *Outline of* Three Meals a Day

The first and second worksheets provide an easy framework for beginning outlining. As your students read the passage, have them underline the information they might include in the outline.   Then, have them fill in the blanks on the prepared outline from information in the passage.   Repeat this task, if necessary, using reading material familiar to your students.

Outlining for Your Health   Name _____

Read the following paragraphs about meals.   Complete the outline on the next page.   Be sure to ask your teacher for help, if you need it.

Three Times a Day

Eating is something most people do at least three times each day.   The main meals are breakfast, lunch, and dinner.   You chose certain kinds of foods for these meals.

Breakfast is the morning meal.   The meal can include eggs, bacon, ham, cereal, bread, or fruit.

Lunch is the meal eaten halfway through the day.   Many people like to eat foods such as soup, salad, and sandwiches.

The evening meal, dinner, is usually the largest meal of the day.   People may eat a main dish of meat or fish.   They may also have salads, vegetables, and rice or bread.

You can eat a light snack or a feast for any of these meals.   The important things to remember are to eat healthful food, and not to eat too much!

Outline of *Three Times a Day*   Name _____

Three Times a Day

A.   Three main meals
   1.   **Breakfast**
   2.   **Lunch**
   3.   **Dinner**
B.   Special foods for each meal
   1.   Breakfast
      a.   **Eggs**
      b.   **Bacon**
      c.   **Ham**
      d.   **Cereal**
      e.   **Bread**
      f.   **Fruit**
   2.   Lunch
      a.   **Soup**
      b.   **Salad**
      c.   **Sandwiches**
   3.   Dinner
      a.   **Meat or fish**
      b.   **Salad**
      c.   **Vegetable**
      d.   **Rice or bread**
C.   Watch what you eat
   1.   **Eat healthful food**
   2.   **Don't eat too much**

Worksheet: *More Outlining*

The last worksheet provides a high-interest passage to be read by your students. Underlining is helpful, but optional. After reading the passage, have your students make an outline on the back of the page. Allow them to review the passage, but consider putting a time restriction (20 minutes) on the preparation of the outline.

More Outlining   Name _____

What is a ''green thumb''? Read the following paragraphs. Then, outline ''A Green Thumb'' on a separate piece of paper. As you read, you'll learn that a ''green thumb'' is a person who is good at making plants grow.

A Green Thumb

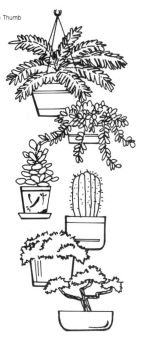

Growing plants in your home can be a fun hobby. If you follow a few simple rules, you can make a room look like a jungle!

To start your plant collection, pick plants that are easy to grow. Some plants can live through almost anything. Philodendrons, ivy, and spider plants are good ''starter'' plants. The plants that you choose should be healthy and bug-free.

There are only three basic rules to follow for growing houseplants. First, make sure the plants get the right amount of light. Most plants need at least four hours of sunlight a day. A north or south window is usually fine for most houseplants. The second rule has to do with watering your plants. To check if your plants need watering, poke your finger in the pot. If the soil is wet, wait for a few days. If the soil is very dry, water it well.

Finally, plants need food just like people do. A garden store will sell you the right houseplant food. Feed or fertilize your plants about once a month.

Remember that houseplants depend on you for everything. By following these simple rules, you will be able to grow happy, healthy houseplants.

WORKSHEET   75

A Green Thumb

A. Starting a plant collection

    1. Easy to grow

    2. Healthy

    3. Bug-free

B. Three basic rules

    1. Give the right amount of light

    2. Water when soil is dry

    3. Feed or fertilize once a month

4 Parts to an Outline

60   Outlining is a great way to organize and remember what you hear or read.   *Outlining* means to write information in order, from the most important to the least important. This ordering of information can help you study for tests, take notes in class, and write reports.

61   First, let's learn the important parts of an outline.

An outline always has a **title**.   The title tells you what the outline is about.

A **main topic** is a very important idea.   Main topics in an outline are like the headings in your textbooks or notes.

A **subtopic** is an idea that's not as important as the main topic.   Subtopics give more information about the main topics.

A **detail** is an extra piece of information.   Details help make the information clearer.

62   You can write an outline in sentences or phrases.   Writing an outline in phrases is shorter and easier.

63   An easy way to remember how to write an outline is to think of building a house.   You start building with the biggest, most important pieces.   You finish with the detail, the little pieces that are not as important to the building.   Let's look at an example of an outline...for building a house!

Building a House ⎯⎯⎯⎯⎯⎯⎯⎯⎯⎯⎯⎯→ Title

  A.   Begin with basement ⎯⎯⎯⎯⎯⎯⎯→ Main Topic
      1.   Dig hole ⎯⎯⎯⎯⎯⎯⎯⎯⎯⎯→ Subtopic
      2.   Line hole with cement ⎯⎯⎯⎯⎯→ Subtopic

  B.   Build supporting walls and floors ⎯⎯→ Main Topic
      1.   Lay boards for floors ⎯⎯⎯⎯⎯→ Subtopic
      2.   Connect floors and ceilings with wallboards ⎯⎯→ Subtopic

  C.   Finish walls and floors⎯⎯⎯⎯⎯⎯→ Main Topic
      1.   Cover wallboards with plaster ⎯⎯→ Subtopic
      2.   Cover floor boards with wood ⎯⎯→ Subtopic

  D.   Finish outside of house ⎯⎯⎯⎯⎯→ Main Topic
      1.   Cover roof with shingles ⎯⎯⎯⎯→ Subtopic
      2.   Cover sides with wood or brick⎯⎯→ Subtopic
         a.   Add shutters to windows⎯⎯⎯→ Detail
         b.   Add front and back doors ⎯⎯⎯→ Detail

Building a house is like building an outline.   You start with the biggest, most important information.   You end with the smallest, least important information.

Horsing Around with Outlining

Name _____

Now, read the following paragraphs. On the next page, you will see how the information you read can be outlined.

Horses

Horses are one of the most helpful animals to man. They are useful for traveling long distances. Horses are strong runners with long legs and hooves designed for running. Horses help people hunt for food, too. Horses have a good sense of smell. They also follow commands well. Many horses are good work animals, especially for farming. They have good memories and learn very quickly.

A horse's coat grows thick every winter. The horse sheds the extra hair every spring. The horse's coat comes in many colors. The horse's coat, mane, and tail make the animal beautiful and warm.

Outline of *Horses*   Name _____

How would you make an outline for Horses?   Here's an example for you.   This outline makes it easy to see the important information quickly.

Horses

  A. Helpful to man

      1. Traveling long distances

          a. Strong runners

          b. Long legs

          c. Hooves for running

      2. Hunting for food

          a. Good sense of smell

          b. Follow commands well

      3. Good workers

          a. Farming

          b. Good memories

          c. Learn quickly

  B. How a horse looks

      1. Coat

          a. Thick in winter for warmth

          b. Sheds in spring for coolness

      2. Color

          a. Comes in many colors

          b. Coat, mane, tail color make it beautiful

Outline of *Seasons of the Year*

Name _____

Here's another example of outlining.   Look how each paragraph on the left has been outlined on the right.   Notice how the outline lists the main ideas describing each season.

Seasons of the Year

There are four seasons of the year. Winter is the first season.   The temperatures are the coldest of the year in winter.   There are many wintertime activities in those parts of the world that have snow and ice. People of all ages can go sledding, skiing, or skating on the ice and snow.

Spring is the second season of the year.   The weather in spring is mild and the temperatures become warmer. Families enjoy having picnics on the new green grass and playing baseball and soccer at the parks.

Seasons of the Year

A.   Winter

    1.   First season of year

    2.   Weather

        a.   Coldest temperatures of year

        b.   Snow and ice

    3.   Activities

        a.   Sledding

        b.   Skating

        c.   Skiing

B.   Spring

    1.   Second season of year

    2.   Weather

        a.   Mild

        b.   Warmer

    3.   Activities

        a.   Picnics

        b.   Baseball

        c.   Soccer

71

Summer is the third season of the year. Summer weather is the hottest of the year. In some places, the air is dry. In others, it is humid or damp. Families cool off by swimming at the beach or city pool. Many people stay inside in the air-conditioning. Those who don't mind the heat play baseball.

C. Summer

   1. Third season of the year

   2. Weather

      a. Hottest temperatures of year

      b. Dry

      c. Humid

   3. Activities

      a. Swimming

      b. Inside in air-conditioning

      c. Baseball

Fall is the fourth season of the year. In the fall, the weather cools off and the first frost arrives. The leaves begin to change colors. People wear warmer clothes to go on walks or to football games.

D. Fall

   1. Fourth season of year

   2. Weather

      a. Cool

      b. First frost

   3. Activities

      a. Walking

      b. Football

Outlining for Your Health

Name _____

Read the following paragraphs about meals. Complete the outline on the next page. Be sure to ask your teacher for help, if you need it.

Three Times a Day

Eating is something most people do at least three times each day. The main meals are breakfast, lunch, and dinner. You chose certain kinds of foods for these meals.

Breakfast is the morning meal. The meal can include eggs, bacon, ham, cereal, bread, or fruit.

Lunch is the meal eaten halfway through the day. Many people like to eat foods such as soup, salad, and sandwiches.

The evening meal, dinner, is usually the largest meal of the day. People may eat a main dish of meat or fish. They may also have salads, vegetables, and rice or bread.

You can eat a light snack or a feast for any of these meals. The important things to remember are to eat healthful food, and not to eat too much!

Outline of *Three Times a Day*   Name _____

Three Times a Day

A.   Three main meals

    1.   _____

    2.   _____

    3.   _____

B.   Special foods for each meal

    1.   Breakfast

        a.   _____

        b.   _____

        c.   _____

        d.   _____

        e.   _____

        f.   _____

    2.   Lunch

        a.   _____

        b.   _____

        c.   _____

    3.   Dinner

        a.   _____

        b.   _____

        c.   _____

        d.   _____

C.   Watch what you eat

    1.   _____

    2.   _____

What is a "green thumb"?   Read the following paragraphs.   Then, outline "A Green Thumb" on a separate piece of paper.   As you read, you'll learn that a "green thumb" is a person who is good at making plants grow.

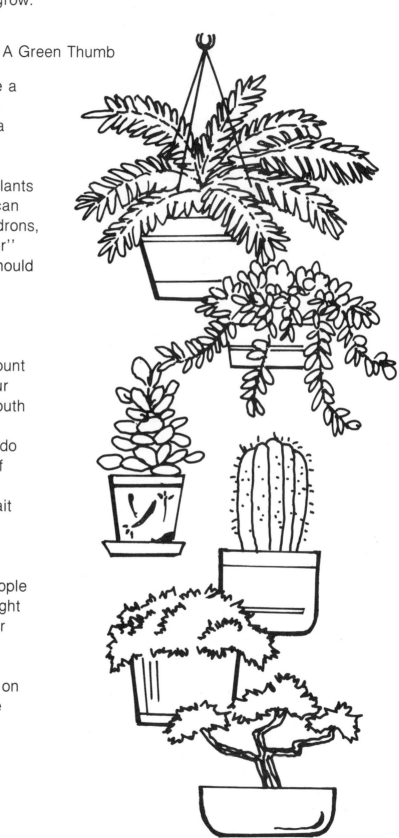

A Green Thumb

Growing plants in your home can be a fun hobby.   If you follow a few simple rules, you can make a room look like a jungle!

To start your plant collection, pick plants that are easy to grow.   Some plants can live through almost anything. Philodendrons, ivy, and spider plants are good "starter" plants.   The plants that you choose should be healthy and bug-free.

There are only three basic rules to follow for growing houseplants.   First, make sure the plants get the right amount of light.   Most plants need at least four hours of sunlight a day.   A north or south window is usually fine for most houseplants.   The second rule has to do with watering your plants.   To check if your plants need watering, poke your finger in the pot.   If the soil is wet, wait for a few days.   If the soil is very dry, water it well.

Finally, plants need food just like people do.   A garden store will sell you the right houseplant food.   Feed or fertilize your plants about once a month.

Remember that houseplants depend on you for everything.   By following these simple rules, you will be able to grow happy, healthy houseplants.

WORKSHEET   75

TAKING NOTES

Now that your students have learned to outline, they are ready to learn the art of note-taking. It is likely that your students already have some good note-taking habits, but they may also need improvement in some areas. This chapter stresses 12 critical factors for note-taking, and assumes that students will get the practice they need by taking notes in class, by preparing for reports,

```
1 handout (pages 79-80)
1 worksheet (page 81)
```

and by rewriting their notes for study purposes.

Handout: *12 Tips for Top-Notch Note-Taking*

This handout stresses the four basic concepts necessary for learning the art of taking notes:

> mental and physical preparation
>
> good listening and concentration
>
> the ability to sort relevant and irrelevant information
>
> good outlining skills

As you present this handout, talk to your students about these four concepts. Keep them "in front" of your students by posting them on the board. If your students can remember these concepts, the 12 tips will seem logical and useful.

Worksheet: *Taking Notes by Outlining*

This worksheet provides your students with note-taking practice on three short passages below. If they need more practice, have them take notes on brochures, magazine articles, newspaper articles, and other chapters of this book. You may find that your students are better at taking notes from material they read than from material they hear. If so, present oral passages from material they've already read, and progress to new and longer oral passages. The ultimate goal should be your students' ability to take notes during all classes and from their textbooks.

Taking Notes by Outlining   Name _____

Your teacher will read each paragraph. Write down the main topic and several subtopics your teacher says. Remember, being a good listener is half the battle!

A.   Dog racing _____

    1. Began in Egypt _____

    2. Most popular in England _____

    3. 30 tracks in U.S. _____

B.   Gymnastic training _____

    1. Training begins young _____

    2. Daily practice _____

    3. Must give up other activities _____

C.   Clothing materials from sheep _____

    1. Greatest producers of materials for clothing _____

    2. Wool ——→ yarn ——→ cloth

    3. Hide ——→ leather

WORKSHEET   81   Copyright 1987 LinguiSystems, Inc.

Have your students listen while you read each paragraph below.   Ask them to write down the most important idea of the reading.   Then, have them write three supporting details to go with each topic.

A.   I'm going to talk about dog racing.

The sport of dog racing began in Egypt long ago.   Today, dog racing is most popular in England.   In the United States, there are about thirty dog racing tracks.

    1.   Dog racing

        a.   Began in Egypt

        b.   Most popular in England

        c.   U.S. — thirty tracks

B.   I'm going to be talking about gymnastics training.

Famous gymnasts usually begin training at a very young age.   Some may begin as early as three years old.   As they get older, they devote more and more time to their training.   They practice every day for many hours.   These long hours of practice mean they must give up many other activities.

    1.   Gymnastics training

        a.   Training — begin young

        b.   Daily practice

        c.   Must give up other activities

C.   I'm going to talk about producing clothing material from sheep.

One of the greatest animal-producers of material for clothing is the sheep.   We use its wool and hides.   Wool from sheep is spun into yarn.   The yarn is turned into cloth.   The tanned hides are used to make beautiful leather.

    1.   Clothing materials from sheep

        a.   Greatest producers of materials for clothing

        b.   Wool ⟶ yarn ⟶ cloth

        c.   Hide ⟶ leather

12 Tips for Top-Notch Note-Taking

Name _____

Taking notes during class helps you to remember what the teacher said.   Your notes will help you study later.   Here are some helpful hints for taking good notes.

64   Get yourself ready before the teacher starts class.   Have your paper, pen, and eraser ready.   Put everything you don't need out of the way.

65   Keep your mind on what the teacher is saying.   Try not to look at or think of anything else.

66   Write down the topic of the material as soon as the teacher says it.

67   Listen for important ideas the teacher says.   Then, write them in your own words.

68   Is the information you're hearing new to you?   If it's not new, you probably don't need to write it down.

69   Don't write every word the teacher says.   Write only a few important words or phrases to help you remember the information.

70   You don't need to write unimportant words, such as *the, a,* and *is.*   These words do not help you understand information better.

71   Use abbreviations or codes to help you go faster.   Here are some suggestions:

e.g.	for example
≈	approximately, about, around, almost
→	to something
←	from something
↔	to and from
w/	with
w/o	without
@	about, at
initials	U.S.A. (United States of America) J.F.K. (John Fitzgerald Kennedy)
re:	regarding, about
etc.	et cetera, and so forth

=	equals
b/c	because
b/t	between

72   Use your outlining skills to take your notes.   Remember, they don't have to be perfect!

73   Rewrite your notes the same day you take them.   Rewriting helps you organize better.   It's also great for learning and remembering the information.

74   Listen for these and other key words from your teacher: "One factor," "Another thing," "There are three ways to do this," "Finally," "An important point is," "Remember," etc.

75   Listen to your teacher's voice.   Louder words are often important to write down and remember.

Now, let's see an example of note-taking.   Suppose you hear this information:

"Today, we are going to talk about things that can help you study.   First, think about the time of day you study.   Study at your own best time: right after school, at night after dinner, or early in the morning.   Next, decide where you'll study.   Maybe you can find a quiet place where no one will bother you.   Last, organize your work area.   Make sure all your materials are in one place.   Then, you won't have to keep getting up for things you need.   I'm sure you can use these suggestions to help you study."

If you had taken notes, they would look something like this:

A.   Things to help my studying

    1.   Best time of day

    2.   Best place

    3.   Organize materials in work area

You're already organized.   Now, get ready to write down some good notes!

Taking Notes by Outlining

Name _____

Your teacher will read each paragraph. Write down the main topic and several subtopics your teacher says. Remember, being a good listener is half the battle!

A. _____

    3. _____

    2. _____

    3. _____

B. _____

    1. _____

    2. _____

    3. _____

C. _____

    1. _____

    2. _____

    3. _____

FOLLOWING ORAL DIRECTIONS

S tudents' difficulty with following oral directions is probably the behavior teachers
consistently cite as most troublesome to their
students' classroom performance.   Poor
listening, further defined as poor <u>critical</u> listening, is what teachers often correctly assume
to be the cause of oral direction-following difficulty.   Therefore, this chapter is devoted to

> 1 handout (pages 87-88)
> 4 worksheets (pages 89-92)

emphasizing concrete techniques to improve
listening for following oral directions.

Handout: *9 Facts about Following Oral Directions*

This handout stresses two simple concepts: listening for important words, and depending
on visual reminders vs. depending on memory.   Again, keep these two important concepts
"in front" of your students as you progress through this handout and the worksheets.

Worksheet: *Listen and Draw*

This first worksheet gives your students a
chance to experience early listening
success.   This is a fun activity to which
students will respond well.   Present the
directions below at a normal, conversa-
tional speaking rate.   Use normal inflection.
Repeat each instruction once.   Pause
after each instruction to give your students
time to complete each instruction before
going on.

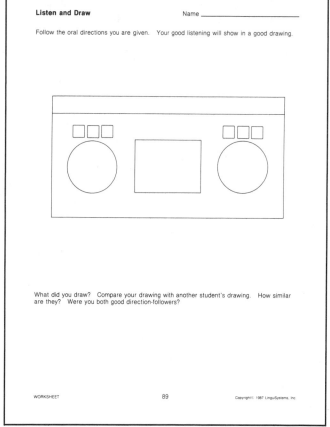

*I am going to give you directions to draw a
picture.   Listen carefully.   I will repeat
each direction once.   Ready?   Let's go!*

1.   *In the middle of your paper, draw a
      rectangle.   It should be about 7
      inches long and 3 inches high.*

2.   *In the middle of your rectangle,
      draw a smaller rectangle.   It should
      be about 2 inches long and 1½
      inches high.*

3.   *On either side of the small
      rectangle, draw a circle.   Each
      circle should be about 1½ inches in diameter.*

4.   *Above each circle, draw 3 very small squares, about the size of a telephone push-
      button.*

5.   *Next, look at the top of the big rectangle.   Draw a half-inch vertical line at each end
      of the rectangle.*

6.   *Last, connect those two lines with one long, straight, horizontal line.*

7.   *What did you draw? (answer: jam box)*

Worksheet: *Ready, Set, Go!*

This second worksheet represents typical worksheet directions from your students' curricula.   Read these directions to your students.   They will need a ruler for this task.   Wait for students to complete instructions before going to the next set of directions.

1. *Look over your math worksheet.*

2. *On your worksheet, do the even numbered problems.   Then, circle your answers.*

3. *In the space below the problems, you will do two drawings.   The first one should be a rectangle.   The horizontal sides should be three inches long and the vertical sides should be one inch long.*

4. *The second drawing at the bottom is a triangle.   The bottom should be about two centimeters.   The two matching sides should be about three centimeters.*

5. *On the bottom of your worksheet, write down the information you need from the following word problem.   Then, solve the problem.   Circle your answer.*

    Mr. Smith drives a total of thirty miles to and from work each day.   He works five days each week.   How many miles does he drive each week?

Were parts of these directions easy for you?   Were others harder?   If you had trouble with any of these directions, let's talk about why.

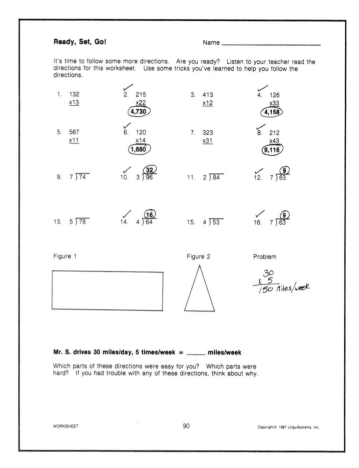

84

Worksheet: *Math Magic*

This third worksheet provides more practice with the following moderately complex oral directions. Read these directions to your students. Wait for them to complete each instruction before going on to the next set of directions.

1. *Look over the ten problems on your worksheet.*

2. *Only work the six problems with the numbers one through six written below the answer boxes.*

3. *Letters of the alphabet have been assigned to the answers of the problems you solved.*

4. *Put the letters for the answers of the problems you solved in the circles at the bottom of the page in the order of one through six.*

5. *Do the letters spell a word you know? (answer: LISTEN)*

Were parts of these directions hard for you? Think about why you made mistakes or had trouble. Think about what you could do differently in the future.

Math Magic   Name _____

You're getting better at direction-following, aren't you? Now, listen to your teacher read some directions out loud. Be sure to write, mark, or draw the directions. They're tricky.

(6 x 3) + 1 = [19] S
3

27 ÷ 3 = [9] I
2

(6 x 1) − 2 = [ ] F
7

(5 x 4) + 2 = [ ] A
8

½ of 40 = [20] T
4

(5 x 5) × 5 = [125] E
5

10 + 10 + 10 = [ ] O
10

(3 x 5) + 10 = [ ] R
9

(7 x 3) − 7 = [14] N
6

6 x 2 = [12] L
1

(L) (I) (S) (T) (E) (N)
 1   2   3   4   5   6

What word do the circles spell? __LISTEN__

Good for you for following all or part of these directions!

Were parts of these directions hard for you? Think about why you made mistakes or had trouble. Then, decide what you could do differently in the future.

Worksheet: *Following Directions with the Word Wizard*

The last worksheet gives your students practice with following oral directions which are grammar-related. Read these directions to your students. Wait for them to complete each instruction before going on to the next step.

1. *Choose an article,* the, an, *or* a, *and write it in the third blank.*

2. *In the seventh blank, write another article,* the, an, *or* a.

3. *Think of two common nouns. Write one common noun in the fifth blank, and the other common noun in the eighth blank.*

4. *Choose a proper noun and write the word in the first blank.*

5. *Think of an action verb. Write the action verb in the second blank.*

6. *Write an adjective in the fourth blank.*

7. *Choose a preposition. Write the preposition in the sixth blank.*

8. *Proofread or check your work.*

Following Directions with the Word Wizard   Name _____

Do you like word games? Listen to your teacher read some directions to you. This word game will be fun and show your direction-following abilities.

(proper noun)	(action)	(article)	(adj.)
1. __Albert__	2. __saw__	3. __an__	4. __old__

(noun)	(preposition)	(article)	(noun)
5. __porch__	6. __on__	7. __the__	8. __river__

The Word Wizard Wonders . . .

What was easy about these directions? __I had time to finish each part.__

What was hard about these directions? __I couldn't think of a proper noun at first.__

Did you make notes to yourself to make the directions easier to follow? __Yes__

Did the notes you took make it possible to check your work? __Yes__   If so, how? __I could check my answers to be sure I had followed the directions.__

What would make it easier for you to check your work?
__Hearing the directions again after I wrote my answers.__

WORKSHEET   92   Copyright© 1987 LinguiSystems, Inc.

Discuss what may have made this set of directions difficult and easy. Did your students have trouble with basic grammar knowledge, the place on the page, or the rate of presentation? Did your students make notes for themselves or clue themselves in order to remember the directions or check their work? When you asked your students to proof their work, was it possible based on clues they recorded on their worksheets?

9 Tips about Following Oral Directions

Name _____

Remembering directions is important, especially for students. Learning to follow directions will help you do work that's correct, complete, and on time. The ideas below will help you to follow directions.

76   Listen for important words. Important words are often words that tell you to do something, such as:

read	decide	do	left
study	center	circle	underline
draw	write	upper	fill-in
listen	remember	tell	choose

77   Listen for numbers. Numbers can tell you what pages to read, how many problems to do, or how many pages to make a report.

78   Listen for words that your teacher repeats or says louder. These words may be important direction-following words.

79   There's a trick to remembering more than one direction at a time. Write numbers and special marks on your worksheets to match what your teacher says. These will help you remember what to do when your teacher is finished giving directions. Look at the page below.

Your teacher gave the following directions:

Write the definitions for the first half of the words.

Then, check your work.

Don't forget to put your name in the upper righthand corner.

You wrote the numbers and marks to remind yourself what to do.

```
Do 1-7        Vocabulary Words   Jim Ryan
 ✓ work
Write the definitions.

 1.  landscape:
 2.  coastline:
 3.  community:
 4.  peninsula:
 5.  island:
 6.  mountain:
 7.  valley:
 8.  river:
 9.  channel:
10.  stream:
11.  border:
12.  capitol:
13.  state:
14.  nation:
```

HANDOUT   87   Copyright© 1987 LinguiSystems, Inc.

80   Picture the directions you hear in your mind.   For example, your teacher says, *Find all the vehicles and circle them.*   In your mind, you see yourself looking at a page, finding the vehicles, and putting a O around each one.

81   Write notes to yourself about the directions you hear, such as:

Find newspaper article.
Outline article.
Prepare oral report.
Due March 10.

82   Sometimes, you can draw the directions you hear.   For example, your teacher says, *Your next report is about litter.   This report should be two pages.   It is due on January 11.   I'd like you to use the article from the January 4* Newsweek *to write your report.*

As your teacher gives you these directions, you draw this:

Litter Report

2 pages.
Due Jan. 11
Use Newsweek
Jan. 4.

83   Repeat the directions to yourself a few times.   Repetition gives you more than one chance to remember what you hear.

84   Don't try to remember directions without writing something down.   You'll be glad you did after a day FULL of directions!

88

Listen and Draw

Name _____

Follow the oral directions you are given.   Your good listening will show in a good drawing.

What did you draw?   Compare your drawing with another student's drawing.   How similar are they?   Were you both good direction-followers?

Ready, Set, Go!

Name _____

It's time to follow some more directions. Are you ready? Listen to your teacher read the directions for this worksheet. Use some tricks you've learned to help you follow the directions.

1. 132
    x13

2. 215
    x22

3. 413
    x12

4. 126
    x33

5. 567
    x11

6. 120
    x14

7. 323
    x31

8. 212
    x43

9. 7$\overline{)74}$

10. 3$\overline{)96}$

11. 2$\overline{)84}$

12. 7$\overline{)63}$

13. 5$\overline{)78}$

14. 4$\overline{)64}$

15. 4$\overline{)53}$

16. 7$\overline{)63}$

Figure 1   Figure 2   Problem

Which parts of these directions were easy for you? Which parts were hard? If you had trouble with any of these directions, think about why.

Math Magic

Name _____

You're getting better at direction-following, aren't you?   Now, listen to your teacher read some directions out loud.   Be sure to write, mark, or draw the directions.   They're tricky.

(6 x 3) + 1 = ☐ S
3

27 ÷ 3 = ☐ I
2

(6 x 1) − 2 = ☐ F
7

(5 x 4) + 2 = ☐ A
8

½ of 40 = ☐ T
4

(5 x 5) × 5 = ☐ E
5

10 + 10 + 10 = ☐ O
10

(3 x 5) + 10 = ☐ R
9

(7 x 3) − 7 = ☐ N
6

6 x 2 = ☐ L
1

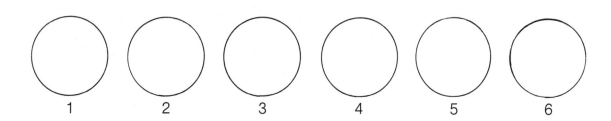

1   2   3   4   5   6

What word do the circles spell? _____

Good for you for following all or part of these directions!

Were parts of these directions hard for you?   Think about why you made mistakes or had trouble.   Then, decide what you could do differently in the future.

Following Directions with the Word Wizard

Do you like word games?   Listen to your teacher read some directions to you.   This word game will be fun and show your direction-following abilities.

1. _____   2. _____   3. _____   4. _____

5. _____   6. _____   7. _____   8. _____

The Word Wizard Wonders . . .

What was easy about these directions? _____

_____

What was hard about these directions? _____

_____

Did you make notes to yourself to make the directions easier to follow? _____

Did the notes you took make it possible to check your work? _____ If so,

how? _____

_____

What would make it easier for you to check your work?

_____

RESPONSIBILITY FOR BEHAVIOR

Many students believe that the trouble they have getting along with adults is the adults' fault. Teachers recognize this factor, too. Although we may not be able to convince our students that part of the responsibility is theirs, we can talk about ways of taking responsibility for getting along. This chapter, Responsibility for Behavior, offers students

---

1 handout (pages 95-96)
3 worksheets (pages 97-100)

---

ready-to-use ways to get along with teachers . . . or any adult, for that matter!

Handout: *18 Magnificent Ways to Manage Your Classroom Behavior*

The handout in this unit stresses the "do's" of showing respect. The 18 ways give your students choices of things to say and behaviors to demonstrate. As you progress through this handout, emphasize the positive attitude change your students and their teachers will see and experience.

Worksheets: *Taking Responsibility for Your Classroom Attitude, Attitude Choices,* and *The Challenger*

All of the worksheets in this chapter present your students with situations to which they must respond as positively as possible. Although the worksheets require written responses, it would be ideal to generate discussion with your students, too, about their responses.

It may take some time for your students to understand and accept the responsibility for their behaviors. (Do we always accept responsibility for our own?!) Therefore, try to avoid using words like *should* and *must,* and substitute words like *can* and *do.*

Students can be dogmatic when they feel "cornered." That is why all of the problems presented ask open-ended questions to get at appropriate solutions. Also, reassure your students that many different answers are acceptable. The point is to avoid limiting answers by being judgmental. Students' answers are solutions which can be added to or modified by you or other students.

Taking Responsibility for Your Classroom Attitude   Name _____

Taking responsibility for how we act is what this worksheet is all about. Read each situation. Each situation could be improved if the student took responsibility for his or her attitude. Write what you think would be a better way to act.

1. Mrs. Perez asks Juan to name the capital of Montana. He stares at her and shrugs his shoulders.

   Juan could say, "I don't know that one."
   _____

2. Joe bothers Lavonna in class by talking to her. Lavonna doesn't answer. Mr. Sheen says, "Lavonna, see me after class." Lavonna says, "I wasn't talking. Joe was."

   Lavonna could wait until after class to explain what happened. Joe could
   help explain to Mr. Sheen.

3. Dana hates French class. She sits in the last row, cleans out her purse, and often is a page or two behind in her book.

   Dana could sit closer to the front, pay attention, and keep up with the class.
   _____

4. Matt's English teacher has just finished a review of all the parts of speech. He did the review quickly because his class has a test tomorrow. Matt doesn't understand prepositions. He says to his English teacher, "This is impossible. I don't understand grammar."

   Matt could ask his teacher to review prepositions with him.
   _____

5. In language arts class, Mr. Williams asks Janice for a set of homonyms. Janice knows what homonyms are, but she can't think of any right now. She answers, "I don't know."

   Janice could say, "I remember homonyms are words that sound the same,
   but I can't think of an example."

WORKSHEET   97   Copyright© 1987 LinguiSystems, Inc.

Attitude Choices   Name _____

Sometimes when we know we're wrong, it's hard to apologize or act polite. That's what we'll practice now. Below are some hard-to-handle situations. Think of the best way to handle each situation. Write your answer in the space provided.

1. You didn't do your homework. Your teacher has just asked you about it. What do you say?

    "I'm sorry. I forgot to do that assignment. I'll do it tonight."

    _____

2. One of your classes is very boring. What is the best way for you to act?

    Pay attention and avoid distractions. Try to find something interesting

    about the class.

3. Your teacher is going too fast. How do you ask your teacher to slow down?

    "I'm sorry, but I can't keep up. Would you go slower, please?"

    _____

4. Your teacher made a mistake and accused you of breaking a class rule. When is the best time for you to talk about the situation with your teacher? What do you say?

    After class I might say, "I think you may have made a mistake. Can we

    talk about what happened?"

5. You are late for class. What do you say to your teacher? When do you say it?

    "I'm sorry I'm late." I'd tell my teacher right away.

    _____

6. You don't understand something your teacher is explaining. How do you let your teacher know?

    I'd raise my hand and say, "I'm confused. Would you explain that again?"

    _____

Attitude Choices, continued   Name _____

7. You lost your homework and gave your teacher an honest explanation. Your teacher still punishes you. What is the best way for you to react?

    Accept the punishment and be more careful with my homework in the future.

    _____

8. You answer in class too often. What can you do about this?

    I could let my classmates raise their hands first for some of the questions.

    _____

9. You feel your teacher has insulted you. You are embarrassed, hurt, and angry. What can you do?

    After class, I could talk to my teacher about my feelings. I could say,

    "I was hurt by your comment today."

10. You want extra help or extra credit. How do you ask for it?

    "I'd like to do some more work for class. What could I do?"

    _____

The Challenger   Name _____

School is full of challenges! Now is your chance to show how you would handle a tough one. Read the situation. Write three or more ways to handle it. Put a star by the best ways you wrote about handling it.

Michael attended the same school for seven years. In that school, he did not get along with Mrs. James. Now, Michael is in seventh grade, and in a new school. He walks into his first class and sees his old teacher, Mrs. James! She has changed schools, too. Michael feels like he wants to run away. What can Michael do to make this a good year for the teacher and himself?

★1. Michael could adopt a positive attitude. He could find things about

    Mrs. James that he likes.

2. Michael could sit near the front and pay attention.

    _____

★3. Michael could walk up to Mrs. James, smile, and say, "Hi! I didn't know

    you changed schools, too!"

4. Michael could avoid direct contact with Mrs. James whenever possible.

    _____

5. Michael could make sure he is on time to class every day.

    _____

6. Michael could try to do his best work for Mrs. James.

    _____

7. _____

    _____

8. _____

    _____

18 Magnificent Ways to Manage Your Classroom Attitude

Name _____

Getting along with your teachers is as important as getting along with your friends. You are kind and polite to your friends. You can be that way with your teachers, too. Here are some ways to show your teachers you're interested in learning. They'll appreciate your positive attitude.

85   Pay attention to your teacher's voice. Notice when your teacher is trying to get your attention by using a louder voice, pausing for a long time, or calling your name.

86   Be interested! Your teacher judges your interest by the way you sit in your chair, by your eye contact, by your appearance, and by your attitude.

87   Raise your hand when you can answer a question or add information. Be sure to stay on the topic being discussed. Keep your comments short and to the point.

88   Ask questions when you need help. These questions will show your teacher that you are interested and paying attention.

89   Some teachers offer special study classes before tests or just to give extra help. If you need the extra help, go to these special classes.

90   Do extra credit work, if your teacher allows it. Extra credit work helps you learn more. Your teacher will be glad you did the extra work.

91   When your teacher offers you help say, ''Thank you.'' Your teacher will appreciate it when you're polite.

92   Answer when you're called on in class. If you don't know the answer, show you were paying attention by saying something like:

    ''I heard your question. I just don't know the answer.''

93   To get ready for class, write down questions you have about the homework, the reading, or your notes. This preparation shows interest on your part. You took time to get ready for class.

94   Avoid sarcasm when you ask or answer questions. Sarcasm is a way of talking which hurts someone's feelings. Sarcasm sounds rude, so don't use it.

95   If the teacher gives an assignment that you think is unfair, don't react right away. Write the assignment down, think about it, and talk about it with one of your parents or another adult. Then, decide what you'll do.

96   Do special things your teacher asks. For example, your teacher may say:

    ''The information you gave on rocks is really interesting. I'd like to see your rock collection.''

Bring your collection the next day. Write it in your assignment book to help you remember. This is a great way to show your interest.

97   Don't make negative comments, such as:

　　　"I can't."
　　　"I don't know how."

　　　Instead, make positive comments, such as:

　　　"I'll try."
　　　"I'm learning."

98   Be honest about your mistakes.   If you forget to do your homework, say so.   Tell your teacher you'll make it up right away, if that's okay.   If it's not okay, accept the outcome.   Make a special effort to remember your homework in the future.

99   Go into your classes a few minutes early.   Being there early will help you get organized.

100   Ask your teacher questions that show your interest, such as:

　　　"Will there be multiple-choice questions?"
　　　"Should we review from the beginning of the year?"

101   Sit toward the front of the class.   Sitting in the front shows your interest and may help you pay attention better.   Don't sit by someone who bothers you.

102   If you have to ask your teacher to slow down or repeat something, ask politely.   Tell your teacher you are having trouble keeping up.

Now, let's see how you can begin showing interest right away.   How about starting today!   Suppose your science teacher is not your favorite teacher.   The two of you just don't get along.   You decide that you're going to get along with your teacher the best you can.   You make these changes right away:

　　　Keep eye contact.
　　　Sit up straight.
　　　Ignore distractions around you.
　　　Take good notes.
　　　Ask questions.
　　　Smile once in a while.
　　　Say good-bye as you leave class.
　　　Come to class a few minutes early each day.
　　　Go to extra study and review sessions.
　　　Get a front row seat.

Suppose your teacher calls on you with a question you can't answer.   To show that you have been paying attention, you say something like:

　　　"I know what you're asking, but I can't think of an example."

Now that you've made these changes, keep up the good work!

96

Taking Responsibility for Your Classroom Attitude

Name _____

Taking responsibility for how we act is what this worksheet is all about.   Read each situation.   Each situation could be improved if the student took responsibility for his or her attitude.   Write what you think would be a better way to act.

1.   Mrs. Perez asks Juan to name the capital of Montana.   He stares at her and shrugs his shoulders.

_____

_____

2.   Joe bothers Lavonna in class by talking to her.   Lavonna doesn't answer.   Mr. Sheen says, "Lavonna, see me after class."   Lavonna says, "I wasn't talking.   Joe was."

_____

_____

3.   Dana hates French class.   She sits in the last row, cleans out her purse, and often is a page or two behind in her book.

_____

_____

4.   Matt's English teacher has just finished a review of all the parts of speech.   He did the review quickly because his class has a test tomorrow.   Matt doesn't understand prepositions.   He says to his English teacher, "This is impossible.   I don't understand grammar."

_____

_____

5.   In language arts class, Mr. Williams asks Janice for a set of homonyms.   Janice knows what homonyms are, but she can't think of any right now.   She answers, "I don't know."

_____

_____

Attitude Choices   Name _____

Sometimes when we know we're wrong, it's hard to apologize or act polite. That's what
we'll practice now. Below are some hard-to-handle situations. Think of the best way to
handle each situation. Write your answer in the space provided.

1. You didn't do your homework. Your teacher has just asked you about it. What do
    you say?

    _____

    _____

2. One of your classes is very boring. What is the best way for you to act?

    _____

    _____

3. Your teacher is going too fast. How do you ask your teacher to slow down?

    _____

    _____

4. Your teacher made a mistake and accused you of breaking a class rule. When is
    the best time for you to talk about the situation with your teacher? What do you
    say?

    _____

    _____

5. You are late for class. What do you say to your teacher? When do you say it?

    _____

    _____

6. You don't understand something your teacher is explaining. How do you let your
    teacher know?

    _____

    _____

7.   You lost your homework and gave your teacher an honest explanation.   Your teacher still punishes you.   What is the best way for you to react?

_____

_____

8.   You answer in class too often.   What can you do about this?

_____

_____

9.   You feel your teacher has insulted you.   You are embarrassed, hurt, and angry.   What can you do?

_____

_____

10.   You want extra help or extra credit.   How do you ask for it?

_____

_____

The Challenger

Name _____

School is full of challenges!   Now is your chance to show how you would handle a tough one.   Read the situation.   Write three or more ways to handle it.   Put a star by the best ways you wrote about handling it.

Michael attended the same school for seven years.   In that school, he did not get along with Mrs. James.   Now, Michael is in seventh grade, and in a new school.   He walks into his first class and sees his old teacher, Mrs. James!   She has changed schools, too.   Michael feels like he wants to run away.   What can Michael do to make this a good year for the teacher and himself?

1. _____

_____

2. _____

_____

3. _____

_____

4. _____

_____

5. _____

_____

6. _____

_____

7. _____

_____

8. _____

_____

TEST PREPARATION

Preparing for a test can be threatening to any student, but especially to those who are not organized or who have waited too long to get started. This chapter on test preparation will give your students six easy-to-understand and very usable strategies to get ready for a test.

1 handout (pages 103-106)
4 worksheets (pages 107-111)

Handout: *6 Ways to Get Ready for a Test*

The handout stresses three essential ideas for success in test preparation:

> reviewing
> every-day-reviewing
> self-testing

Although these essentials may seem overly simplified, they require self-discipline, a quality difficult for many of our students to acquire. Therefore, as you present this handout, repeat these essentials often and in a positive way. These essentials should not be viewed as burdens by your students, but as ways to achieve success on tests.

Worksheets: *Test Yourself, Shaping and Measuring Up, Getting the Bugs Out*, and *Have a Heart!*

All of the worksheets in this chapter require your students to design test questions and provide the correct responses. They need to use their outlining, surveying, and skimming skills as well as to concentrate on following directions.

Other assignments you could provide as supplements to this chapter are:

> rewriting notes and comparing them with the originals,

> writing sample test questions that evaluate the learning of this chapter,

> having students ask questions of each other that evaluate the learning of this chapter, or

> researching test preparation from other references in the school or public library.

Test Yourself   Name _____

Now, here's the real test! Complete the following directions. Be ready to discuss your answers. You'll do a super job!

Make fill-in-the-blank test questions with the following information.

A. In the metric system, the unit for distance is the meter. The unit for volume is the liter. The unit for weight is the gram.

1. __The unit for _____ is the meter.__

2. __The unit for _____ is the liter.__

3. __The unit for _____ is the gram.__

B. Illinois is sometimes called *The Land of Lincoln*. President Lincoln spent his early years as a lawyer in Springfield, the capital of Illinois.

1. _____ is the Land of Lincoln.__

2. __President Lincoln was a _____ of Illinois.__

3. __Springfield is the _____ of Illinois.__

Write true-false questions for the following information.

A. The Nile River is the longest river in the world. It is located in Egypt. The longest river in the United States is the Mississippi River.

True   False   1. __The Mississippi River is the longest river in the world.__

True   False   2. __The Nile River is in Egypt.__

B. The term *flu* is a short name for *influenza*. Symptoms of influenza include chills, fever, headaches, stomach upsets, and aches in the bone joints. Flu affects the whole body.

True   False   1. __"Flu" means "to fly away."__

True   False   2. __Symptoms of influenza are fever and headaches.__

WORKSHEET   107   Copyright© 1987 LinguiSystems, Inc.

Shaping and Measuring Up   Name _____

More self-testing? You bet! Make matching tests from the following information.

A. Shapes

   1. A triangle is a three-sided figure.

   2. A square is a four-sided figure with all sides being equal.

   3. A line is the straight distance between two points.

   4. A rectangle is a four-sided figure with two equal vertical sides and two equal horizontal sides. The vertical and horizontal sides may not be equal. If all four sides are equal, the figure is a square.

Terms		Definitions
a. __triangle__	___	**a four-sided figure with equal sides**
b. __square__	___	**a four-sided figure with equal vertical**
		and equal horizontal sides
c. __line__	___	**a three-sided figure**
d. __rectangle__	___	**the straight distance between two points**

B. Measurements

   1. 12 inches equal 1 foot.

   2. 3 feet equal 1 yard.

   3. 8 ounces equal 1 cup.

   4. 2 cups equal 1 pint.

Terms		Definitions
a. __foot__		**equals 2 cups**
b. __yard__		**equals 8 ounces**
c. __cup__		**equals 3 feet**
c. __pint__		**equals 12 inches**

Getting the Bugs Out   Name _____

Write a short-answer question for each of the following paragraphs. Then, write answers for your questions.

1. Ants are the smartest of all insects. They live in large groups called *colonies*. These colonies have many passages underground. Anthills are only part of the entire colony.

   Question: **Where do ants live?** _____

   Answer: **Ants live in colonies under the ground.** _____

2. Bees are the only insects that produce food eaten by humans. We use bees' honey in cooking and baking, on bread, and as a sweetener in beverages. We also use the wax from their nests to make candles and lipsticks.

   Question: **What do we use honey for?** _____

   Answer: **We use honey for sweetening in cooking and baking.** _____

3. Moths are related to butterflies. They are less brightly colored. Moths usually fly at night and may eat holes in wool clothes.

   Question: **Name a way that moths are different from butterflies.** _____

   Answer: **Moths are less brightly colored than butterflies.** _____

Have a Heart!   Name _____

Suppose the notes below are from your science class. After you've read these notes, go to the next page and follow the directions.

A. Circulatory System

   1. Vocabulary

     a. Ventricles — pumping "houses"

     b. Arteries — carry blood away from the heart

     c. Veins — carry blood to the heart

     d. White blood cells — fight infection and destroy bacteria

     e. Hemoglobin — red protein that joins with oxygen

     f. Red blood cells — carry oxygen through the body

   2. Facts

     a. When blood reaches the lungs, it picks up oxygen.

     b. Hemoglobin is found in red blood cells.

     c. A pulse can be felt only in the arteries.

   3. Parts of the heart

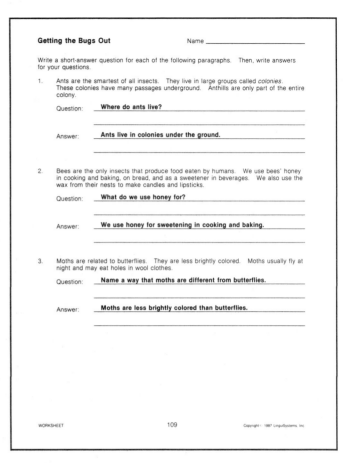

left atrium   right atrium

vein   valve

left ventricle   right ventricle

Have a Heart!, continued   Name _____

B. Write a "listing" question about the vocabulary.

   List six parts of the heart. _____

C. Write three true-false questions about the blood.

  True   False   1.   **Arteries carry blood to the heart.** _____

  True   False   2.   **A pulse can be found only in veins.** _____

  True   False   3.   **Red blood cells carry oxygen through the body.** _____

D. Write four fill-in-the-blank questions about the circulatory system.

   1.   **The** _____ **blood cells fight infection and destroy bacteria.**

   2.   **Blood picks up oxygen when it reaches the** _____ .

   3.   _____ **is a red protein that joins with oxygen in the blood.**

   4.   _____ **carry blood away from the heart.**

E. Write two multiple-choice questions about the parts of the heart.

   1.   Question: **Which one carries blood to the heart?**

       Answers: **ventricle** ___ **vein** ___ **artery**

   2.   Question: **Which one fights disease and bacteria?**

       Answers: **red blood cells** ___ **hemoglobin** ___ **white blood cells**

6 Ways to Get Ready for a Test

Name _____

Do you know how to get ready for a test?   Begin studying even before you find out you're going to have a test!   Really?   Really!   Preparing for a test means studying for the test every day.   Every day?   Yes!   But, it's easy.   Just remember that studying is learning information you already have written down. So, every day:

103   Reread notes in your notebooks.   Repetition is the best way to learn.

104   Rewrite notes in your notebook.   This repetition will help, too.

105   Add information to your notes that you may find while reading your textbook.

106   Skim textbook material covered that day.

107   Highlight or underline while you skim.   You can also underline your notes.

Rereading your notes, rewriting your notes, and skimming your textbook will take five to ten minutes for each subject each night.   This overviewing is in addition to your regular homework.   But don't worry.   With good planning, you can still have time to watch TV and talk on the phone!

108   What else can you do to get ready for a test?   You've studied every day.   Now what?   How about testing yourself?   Self-testing is a good way to get ready for a test.

Test yourself about a week before the test.   Then, continue studying.   Test yourself once more the day before the test.

To test yourself, write down questions you think your teacher might ask.   You can think of the questions by reviewing your notes or your textbook.

Now that you've written questions, answer them!   Try to answer them without looking at your book or notes.   Answer your own questions out loud, with a tape recorder, or in writing.   Make sure you check your answers by listening to the tape or comparing your written answers to your notes or book.

Try having someone else ask you questions about the material.   They can ask questions from your notes or from your textbook.

A study group is another way to self-test.   Get together with two or three other students to talk about the material.   You can ask each other questions, or discuss what you've learned.

Spend most of your self-testing time on the hardest material.   Be sure you plan this time on your calendar.

Learning how to self-test for different kinds of tests is important.   Self-testing for an essay test is different than self-testing for a multiple-choice test.   Let's check out the differences.

For math, you will probably have to work problems.   Study by practicing several problems.   Have an adult check your work, or check your work against the answer section if your textbook has one.

Grammar tests often have matching and fill-in-the blank questions.   Tests about books you've read often have short-answer questions and essay questions.   To study, go over your notes on grammar or the book you've read.

One way to study for spelling or vocabulary tests is to divide a page in half vertically.   On one side, write the words.   On the other side, write the definitions.   Test yourself by folding the sheet and filling in either the words or the definitions out loud or by writing on a separate piece of paper.   Finally, compare your work with the original sheet.   Or, test yourself on the spelling or definitions out loud using a tape recorder.   Replay the tape and listen to your answers.   Your paper might look like this:

Words	Definitions
1. island	a body of land surrounded by water
2. coastline	the land or shore by an ocean or lake
3. river	a narrow body of fresh water that flows into a lake or an ocean.

Fill-in-the-blank and multiple-choice questions are found on science, history, and social studies tests.   To study for these tests, write the questions on the left and the answers on the right.   Fold the paper to test yourself.   Your paper might look like this:

1. The planets revolve around the _____.	Sun
2. The closest planet to the sun is _____.	Mercury
3. The farthest planet from the sun is _____.	Pluto

Or, your paper might look like this:

1. Name the planets.	Mercury Venus Earth Mars Jupiter Saturn Uranus	Neptune Pluto

Now, let's try some self-testing from your class notes.   Suppose your notes from science look like this:

A.   Planets

1.   Bodies revolving around the sun

2.   Patterns of revolution — fairly regular

3.   Order closest to the sun
   a.   Mercury
   b.   Venus
   c.   Earth
   d.   Mars
   e.   Jupiter
   f.   Saturn
   g.   Uranus
   h.   Neptune
   i.   Pluto

4.   Characteristics
   a.   Rotate
   b.   Round

After reviewing these notes, you make up study questions like the following:

1.   What are planets?

2.   Name the planets, beginning with the closest to the sun.

3.   Which planet is probably the hottest?

4.   Which planet is probably the coldest?

5.   List three characteristics of planets.

Answer these questions aloud with a tape recorder, or write your answers.   You may want to do both.   Next, compare your answers to your textbook or your notes.   Remember to spend the most time on the hardest material.

Here's another self-test.

Your history teacher has talked about the Civil War for five days.   You have many notes.   You find out the test will be an essay test.   Write some questions and answer them with facts.   List your answers.   Then, write a paragraph to answer each of your questions.

1.   What were the causes of the Civil War?
   A.   Slavery
   B.   North vs. South
   C.   The breakup of the Union

   The Civil War was caused by the North and South disagreeing about slavery.   The North wanted slavery to end.   The South kept slaves to run their plantations.   Some states could not agree whether to keep slaves or not.   Those who wanted to keep slaves finally decided to form their own country.

2.   What part did President Lincoln play in the Civil War?
   A.   Freed the slaves
   B.   Commander in Chief
   C.   Tried to keep the country together

   When Lincoln became President, he freed the slaves.   The South was upset.   They formed their own country.   President Lincoln was the Commander in Chief in the North.   He said it was his job to keep the country together.   He didn't want a war.   He wanted one strong country.

Test Yourself   Name _____

Now, here's the real test!   Complete the following directions.   Be ready to discuss your answers.   You'll do a super job!

Make fill-in-the-blank test questions with the following information.

A.   In the metric system, the unit for distance is the meter.   The unit for volume is the liter.   The unit for weight is the gram.

1. _____

2. _____

3. _____

B.   Illinois is sometimes called *The Land of Lincoln*.   President Lincoln spent his early years as a lawyer in Springfield, the capital of Illinois.

1. _____

2. _____

3. _____

Write true-false questions for the following information.

A.   The Nile River is the longest river in the world.   It is located in Egypt.   The longest river in the United States is the Mississippi River.

True   False   1. _____

True   False   2. _____

B.   The term *flu* is a short name for *influenza*.   Symptoms of influenza include chills, fever, headaches, stomach upsets, and aches in the bone joints.   Flu affects the whole body.

True   False   1. _____

True   False   2. _____

Shaping and Measuring Up

Name _____

More self-testing?   You bet!   Make matching tests from the following information.

A.   Shapes

1.   A triangle is a three-sided figure.

2.   A square is a four-sided figure with all sides being equal.

3.   A line is the straight distance between two points.

4.   A rectangle is a four-sided figure with two equal vertical sides and two equal horizontal sides.   The vertical and horizontal sides may not be equal.   If all four sides are equal, the figure is a square.

	Terms		Definitions
a.	_____	____	_____
b.	_____	____	_____
			_____
c.	_____	____	_____
d.	_____	____	_____

B.   Measurements

1.   12 inches equal 1 foot.

2.   3 feet equal 1 yard.

3.   8 ounces equal 1 cup.

4.   2 cups equal 1 pint.

	Terms		Definitions
a.	_____	____	_____
b.	_____	____	_____
c.	_____	____	_____
c.	_____	____	_____

Getting the Bugs Out

Name _____

Write a short-answer question for each of the following paragraphs.   Then, write answers for your questions.

1.   Ants are the smartest of all insects.   They live in large groups called *colonies*.
     These colonies have many passages underground.   Anthills are only part of the entire
     colony.

     Question: _____

     _____

     Answer: _____

     _____

2.   Bees are the only insects that produce food eaten by humans.   We use bees' honey
     in cooking and baking, on bread, and as a sweetener in beverages.   We also use the
     wax from their nests to make candles and lipsticks.

     Question: _____

     _____

     Answer: _____

     _____

3.   Moths are related to butterflies.   They are less brightly colored.   Moths usually fly at
     night and may eat holes in wool clothes.

     Question: _____

     _____

     Answer: _____

     _____

Have a Heart!   Name _____

Suppose the notes below are from your science class.   After you've read these notes, go to
the next page and follow the directions.

A. Circulatory System

   1. Vocabulary

       a. Ventricles — pumping "houses"

       b. Arteries — carry blood away from the heart

       c. Veins.— carry blood to the heart

       d. White blood cells — fight infection and destroy bacteria

       e. Hemoglobin — red protein that joins with oxygen

       f. Red blood cells — carry oxygen through the body

   2. Facts

       a. When blood reaches the lungs, it picks up oxygen.

       b. Hemoglobin is found in red blood cells.

       c. A pulse can be felt only in the arteries.

   3. Parts of the heart

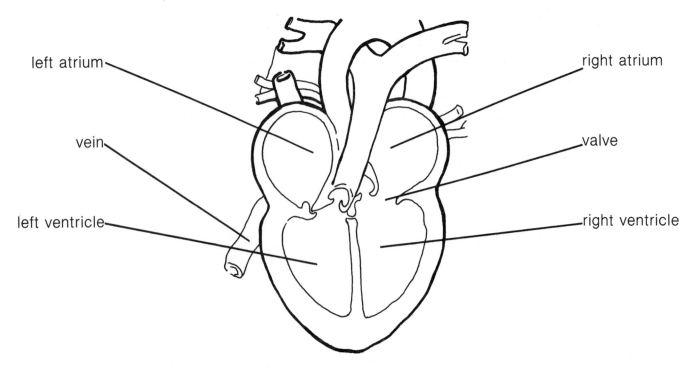

left atrium

right atrium

vein

valve

left ventricle

right ventricle

B.   Write a "listing" question about the vocabulary.

_____

_____

C.   Write three true-false questions about the blood.

True   False   1. _____

_____

True   False   2. _____

_____

True   False   3. _____

_____

D.   Write four fill-in-the-blank questions about the circulatory system.

1. _____

_____

2. _____

_____

3. _____

_____

4. _____

_____

E.   Write two multiple-choice questions about the parts of the heart.

1.   Question: _____

Answers: _____

2.   Question: _____

Answers: _____

TEST-TAKING

Now, the heat is on. Your students are bent over their tests, some with determination, some with anticipation, but all, hopefully, with confidence.

This chapter on test-taking is intended to give your students the strategies they need to take tests confidently and well. Besides these strategies, though, your students need a healthy dose of self-discipline to apply the strategies. Perhaps having concrete suggestions to follow is what our students need to generate the real desire to succeed.

1 handout (pages 117-119)
3 worksheets (pages 120-125)

Handout: *10 Ways to Ace a Test*

This handout stresses the following principles of successful testing:

    overviewing or surveying
    planning
    working at a steady pace

Often, our students jump right into a test without looking it over, planning which questions to answer first, or keeping a steady rate of responding. As a result, they may skip questions they meant to answer, spend too much time on a few questions, or answer incorrectly. The ten strategies in this handout discuss ways to avoid these test-taking pitfalls.

Worksheet: *"Testing, Testing . . ."*

This first worksheet is meant to give your students practice in taking a test with many question formats. Although the information is easy, there are a few items that are intentionally difficult. These are used to train your students' process of elimination. If any of the information is inappropriate, substitute more appropriate subject matter into the same formats.

"Testing, Testing . . ." Name _____

Are you ready to practice taking a test? Read and follow the directions carefully. This will be a snap!

A. Circle the letter of the best answer. Put a star by the question you answer first.

1. We live on the planet called _____ .

   a. Mars   b. America   c. United States   (d.) Earth

2. The opposite of *day* is _____ .

   (a.) night   b. dark   c. dayless   d. date

3. To make ice cream, you need _____ .

   a. cream   b. sugar   c. salt   (d.) all of these

B. Answer either one of these questions. Do not answer both.

1. List three ways you could get to school.

   a. __by bus__

   b. __by car__

   c. __on my bike__

2. In two complete sentences, describe your feelings about going back to school in the fall.

   _____

   _____

   _____

   _____

C. Write the number of each word on the line next to its correct definition. Do not use word number five.

   ✓1. alliteration   __2__ the opposite of scream

   ✓2. whisper   __4__ what grows on a cat's face

   ✓3. principal   __1__ the use of an initial letter
                                    over and over in words

   ✓4. whisker   __3__ the head of a school

   5. incandescent (crossed out)

WORKSHEET   120   Copyright © 1987 LinguiSystems, Inc.

"Testing, Testing . . .", continued Name _____

D. Write a *T* or an *F* on each blank. If a statement is false, make the statement true.

1. _F_ Milk is always cold. **Milk is sometimes cold.**

2. _F_ Babies never cry, but they sometimes eat. **Babies cry and eat.**

3. _F_ Today is Sunday. **Today is Friday.**

4. _T_ Some houses are made with bricks.

E. What is your city's weather like in the summer? Do not use the word *hot*.

   Our weather is sticky, humid, and damp. People perspire from the heat.

   The temperature goes up into the 90's. People stay inside to keep cool.

   _____

   _____

   _____

   _____

   _____

WORKSHEET   121   Copyright © 1987 LinguiSystems, Inc.

Worksheet: *Practice Makes Perfect*

The next worksheet gives your students a chance to be ''shining stars.'' If they read the test <u>all</u> <u>the</u> <u>way</u> <u>through</u>, as the instructions say, they'll find out they're not to answer any questions at all! Undoubtedly, some students will begin the test and work feverishly to complete it, as they wonder why the other students have finished so fast. When the test (and fun!) are over, have your students problem-solve as the way to avoid this problem in the future.

Practice Makes Perfect　　　　　　　Name _____

If practice makes perfect, you're on your way! Read this test all the way through before beginning. Be careful!

A. Write the letter of each word on the line next to its correct definition.

1. ____ unhappiness　　　　　a. happiness

2. ____ Alexander the Great's horse　　b. Bucephalus

3. ____ the opposite of *sadness*　　c. sorrow

4. ____ a two-wheeled object for　　d. bicycle
transportation

B. Write a *T* or an *F* on each blank. If a statement is false, turn it into a true one.

1. ____ Some people like ice cream.

2. ____ Cats never sleep, but they sometimes purr.

3. ____ My hair color is brown.

4. ____ Cars are always red.

C. Circle the letter of the best answer.

1. To grow a plant, you need _____ .

a. water　　b. soil　　c. seeds　　d. all of these

2. July 4 is called _____ .

a. Independence Day　b. Christmas Day　c. Easter　d. Halloween

3. A year has _____ months.

a. ten　　b. nine　　c. fifteen　　d. twelve

D. List three things that make you angry.

1. _____

2. _____

3. _____

Practice Makes Perfect, continued　　　　Name _____

E. What is your favorite hobby? Why?

_____

_____

_____

_____

_____

F. Why do people have pets?

_____

_____

_____

_____

_____

_____

_____

_____

G. Do not answer <u>any</u> of the questions on this test. Hand your test in after you read the next question.

H. Did you read the test all the way through before beginning? Good for you! You get an A+ for ABSOLUTELY terrific!

Worksheet: *Your Final Exam*

This last worksheet gives more practice in taking tests containing multiple-choice, true-false, fill-in-the-blank, listing, matching, and essay questions.   If necessary, consider more practice by giving your students tests they've already taken.   They can concentrate more on following the directions and you can compare the results of the first test to the new results.

Your Final Exam   Name _____

Let's try this test-taking one more time.   You're nearly perfect!   Good work!

A. List five steps in making a hamburger.

1. <u>Take a handful of ground beef.</u>
2. <u>Press it between your hands to make a patty.</u>
3. <u>Cook it on both sides in a pan.</u>
4. <u>Put the hamburger on a bun.</u>
5. <u>Put ketchup on it and cover it with the top bun.</u>

B. Define the word *car*.

<u>A car is a vehicle you can drive. It has four wheels, an engine, and can</u>
<u>carry more than one person.</u>

C. Write *T* or *F* on each blank.   If the statement is false, turn it into a true one.

1. <u>F</u> All men in Texas are cowboys.   **Some men in Texas are cowboys.**
2. <u>T</u> Many words have the letter *e* in them.
3. <u>F</u> Cats never sleep in the daytime.   **Cats usually sleep in the daytime.**
4. <u>F</u> Minnesota never has any snow.   **Minnesota has snow in the winter.**

D. Draw a line from each word to its correct definition.

1. carrot   an organ of the body
2. eight   an orange vegetable
3. pancreas   to have eaten
4. ate   a number

Your Final Exam, continued   Name _____

E. Circle the best answer.

1. Sixty-three is the same as _____ .

    a. 68 − 3   b. 821 − 3   (c.) 7 x 9   d. 6 x 8

2. A bicycle has _____ .

    a. two wheels   b. pedals   c. handlebars   (d.) all of these

3. Another word for *cap* is _____ .

    a. cat   (b.) hat   c. dress   d. head

F. Discuss at least two differences and two similarities between apples and oranges.

<u>Apples are red, green or yellow. Oranges are orange. Apples have skin</u>
<u>you can eat. Oranges have skin you can't eat. Apples and oranges are</u>
<u>fruit. They both grow on trees.</u>
_____
_____
_____
_____

10 Ways to Ace a Test

Name _____

How can you do well on a test? You've taken good notes, right? You've studied, right? Then, think of a test as a way of showing how much you know. Once you know what types of tests there are, you'll do better at taking them. Here are some ways that will help you do your best work on tests.

109 Look over the test as soon as your teacher hands it out.

> Read over or skim the entire test.
>
> Read and understand all directions. Mark the directions with a ★.
>
> Look for clue words in directions and questions. Try underlining or circling the most important words.
>
> Notice the kinds of questions and how many points each question is worth.

110 Plan your time by how many points the questions are worth. Do the questions that count the most first.

111 Or, choose the easiest questions to do first. Go back and do the harder ones later. Don't forget to do the ones you skipped. Mark them as you skip them to remind you to go back to them later.

112 Review the entire test before handing it in to the teacher. If you have time, check it twice. Be sure you followed directions and didn't skip anything.

113 Be sure of the scoring method. If your teacher counts off for wrong answers, don't guess. Just do the ones you know and leave the rest.

114 You need to plan carefully for **essay** tests. Here are some great tips.

> Remember to start with the easiest essay questions. Doing the easy questions first will get your mind going. The easiest ones will give you more confidence to go on to the harder questions.
>
> Plan your answers by jotting down important facts first. Do this jotting in the margins or on a separate sheet of paper. Then, add to this information until you've answered the question.
>
> Just answer the question that was asked. Don't add a lot of unimportant information. Begin your answer by restating the question, such as:
>
> What are some snacks that are good for you?
>
> Some snacks that are good for you include peanuts, raw vegetables, fresh fruit, and juice.

Notice the most important words in directions on essay tests, like *trace, compare, contrast, list, discuss*, etc.

Trace means to show what happened from beginning to end.

Compare means to show the things that are the same and the things that are different.

Contrast means to tell how things are different.

Discuss means to write about what you know.

List means to write words or phrases separately.

115   Short-answer tests need your quick, steady work.   Begin with the easiest questions.   Work at a steady pace.   Spend about the same amount of time on each question.   Don't waste time on questions if you don't know the answer.   Put a ★ or a ✔ by the ones you skip, and go back to them later.   For example:

✔A. Name the 9 planets: _____

_____

B. What do all planets do in the solar system?   <u>rotate</u>

C. What shape are all planets?   <u>round</u>

116   Multiple-choice tests need your quick thinking.   Read all the choices for each question.   Then, cross out the answers you know are <u>not</u> right.   Finally, choose the best of the answers you have left.   For example:

A. Ventricles are: (1.) pumping "houses" of the heart

                        2.   blood vessels

                        3.   ~~elbow joints~~

B. Parts of the heart are: 1.   ~~foyer, vestibule, lobby~~

                        (2.) veins, valve, atrium

                        3.   Nina, Pinta, Santa Maria

117 **Matching** tests are fun and fast.   As you use each answer, check it off.   Be careful!   Sometimes, the same answer may be used more than once.   Crossing out answers will help you to see which answers are left.   For example:

    A. 1. island   _3_   a narrow body of fresh water that flows to an ocean or lake

         2. coastline   _2_   the land or shore by an ocean or lake

         3. river   _1_   a body of land surrounded by water

    B. 1. The planets revolve around the   _2_ Mercury

         2. The closest planet to the sun is   _3_ Pluto

         3. The farthest planet from the sun is   _1_ Sun

118 **True-false** tests can be tricky.   Most statements which use words like *always* and *never* are generally false on true-false tests.   Also, if any part of a statement is false, the entire statement is false.   For example:

    A. The North never opposed slavery.   True   (False)

    B. The North wanted to free the slaves.   (True)   False

    C. President Lincoln believed in slavery, but wanted one strong country.   True   (False)

"Testing, Testing . . ."   Name _____

Are you ready to practice taking a test?   Read and follow the directions carefully.   This will be a snap!

A.   Circle the letter of the best answer.   Put a star by the question you answer first.

    1.   We live on the planet called _____ .

        a.   Mars   b.   America   c.   United States   d.   Earth

    2.   The opposite of *day* is _____ .

        a.   night   b.   dark   c.   dayless   d.   date

    3.   To make ice cream, you need _____ .

        a.   cream   b.   sugar   c.   salt   d.   all of these

B.   Answer either one of these questions.   Do not answer both.

    1.   List three ways you could get to school.

        a.   _____

        b.   _____

        c.   _____

    2.   In two complete sentences, describe your feelings about going back to school in the fall.

        _____

        _____

        _____

        _____

C.   Write the number of each word on the line next to its correct definition.   Do not use word number five.

    1.   alliteration   ____ the opposite of scream

    2.   whisper   ____ what grows on a cat's face

    3.   principal   ____ the use of an initial letter over and over in words

    4.   whisker   ____ the head of a school

    5.   incandescent

D. Write a *T* or an *F* on each blank.   If a statement is false, make the statement true.

    1. ____ Milk is always cold.

    2. ____ Babies never cry, but they sometimes eat.

    3. ____ Today is Sunday.

    4. ____ Some houses are made with bricks.

E. What is your city's weather like in the summer?   Do not use the word *hot*.

_____

_____

_____

_____

_____

_____

_____

Practice Makes Perfect   Name _____

If practice makes perfect, you're on your way!   Read this test all the way through before
beginning.   Be careful!

A.   Write the letter of each word on the line next to its correct definition.

   1. ____   unhappiness   a.   happiness

   2. ____   Alexander the Great's horse   b.   Bucephalus

   3. ____   the opposite of *sadness*   c.   sorrow

   4. ____   a two-wheeled object for   d.   bicycle
             transportation

B.   Write a *T* or an *F* on each blank.   If a statement is false, turn it into a true one.

   1. ____   Some people like ice cream.

   2. ____   Cats never sleep, but they sometimes purr.

   3. ____   My hair color is brown.

   4. ____   Cars are always red.

C.   Circle the letter of the best answer.

   1.   To grow a plant, you need _____ .

        a.   water   b.   soil   c.   seeds   d.   all of these

   2.   July 4 is called _____ .

        a.   Independence Day   b.   Christmas Day   c.   Easter   d.   Halloween

   3.   A year has _____ months.

        a.   ten   b.   nine   c.   fifteen   d.   twelve

D.   List three things that make you angry.

   1.   _____

   2.   _____

   3.   _____

Name _____

E. What is your favorite hobby?   Why?

_____

_____

_____

_____

_____

F. Why do people have pets?

_____

_____

_____

_____

_____

_____

G. Do not answer <u>any</u> of the questions on this test.   Hand your test in after you read the next question.

H. Did you read the test all the way through before beginning?   Good for you!   You get an A+ for ABSOLUTELY terrific!

123

Your Final Exam   Name _____

Let's try this test-taking one more time.   You're nearly perfect!   Good work!

A.   List five steps in making a hamburger.

1.   _____

2.   _____

3.   _____

4.   _____

5.   _____

B.   Define the word *car*.

_____

_____

C.   Write *T* or *F* on each blank.   If the statement is false, turn it into a true one.

1.   ____   All men in Texas are cowboys.

2.   ____   Many words have the letter *e* in them.

3.   ____   Cats never sleep in the daytime.

4.   ____   Minnesota never has any snow.

D.   Draw a line from each word to its correct definition.

1.   carrot   an organ of the body

2.   eight   an orange vegetable

3.   pancreas   to have eaten

4.   ate   a number

Name _____

E. Circle the best answer.

1. Sixty-three is the same as _____ .

    a. 68 − 3   b. 821 − 3   c. 7 x 9   d. 6 x 8

2. A bicycle has _____ .

    a. two wheels   b. pedals   c. handlebars   d. all of these

3. Another word for *cap* is _____ .

    a. cat   b. hat   c. dress   d. head

F. Discuss at least two differences and two similarities between apples and oranges.

_____

_____

_____

_____

_____

_____

125

TEST-PROOFING

Test-proofing is a skill that's easy to learn but difficult to carry through. Parents and teachers alike identify proofing of tests, homework, and written reports as sorely lacking in the upper elementary grades and in junior and senior high school. Therefore, formal instruction may be a necessity in this success-oriented strategy.

Handout: *7 Ways to Proofread Your Tests*

The handout in this unit stresses:

rereading
reviewing
redoing

Your students will become aware of different methods of checking for correct answers and checking to make sure directions were followed appropriately. As you progress through this handout, reassure your students that no one expects perfection. Stress that you are interested in improving their proofing skills so that they can use these skills for tests, reports, and note-taking.

Worksheets: *Check-a-Test* and *The Proof Is in the Answers*

Worksheets one and two are designed to have your students correct the mistakes already made. They may need extra help in correcting the answers on the essay questions, since these answers lack information rather than having incorrect information.

1 handout (pages 130-131)
3 worksheets (pages 132-136)

Check-a-Test   Name _____

Do you think you're ready to prove how much you've learned? Suppose that you have just finished this test. Now, check your work. Correct your mistakes.

A. List five characteristics of your school. Each characteristic should be an adjective.

1. big
2. noisy
3. cold
4. ~~I have friends there~~ busy
5. friendly

B. Write *T* for True or *F* for False in each blank. Make true statements false.

___T___ 1. The sun is a star. **The sun is a planet.**

___T___ 2. Air conditioners help keep us cool. **Air conditioners keep us warm.**

C. Write the number of the definition in the blank next to the correct word.

1. coldest season   ___1___ winter
2. leaves turn color   ___4___ spring
3. hottest season   ___3___ summer
4. plants bloom again   2 ___4___ fall

D. Use the following word to complete each statement. Each word may be used more than once.

infants   children   adults

1. People who usually make rules are _adults_
2. People most likely to be in school are _children_
3. People who usually go to work each day are ~~infants~~ **adults**
4. People who most often make their needs known by crying are _infants_
5. People who spend most of their time playing are _infants_

WORKSHEET   132   Copyright© 1987 LinguiSystems, Inc.

127

E. Explain the reasons for the Civil War.   Write at least three sentences.

The Civil War was fought over the idea of slavery.

The North believed slavery was wrong.   The South believed slaves were needed

to run the plantations.   The North and South could not agree.   They fought to

become two countries instead of one.

_____

F. Do you think twelve years of school is enough, too little, or too much?   Tell why you feel as you do in at least three or four sentences.

Yes. **I don't think twelve years of school is enough.   Twelve years only**

gets you through high school.   If you want to learn a special trade, you

have to go to vocational school.   If you don't go to vocational school, you

should go to college.

You're almost ready to try the real thing.   Let's proof one more time!   Suppose you have just finished this test.   Now, check your work.   Correct your mistakes.

A. Write the letter of the definition that matches each word.

1. one of anything   **3**   ~~A~~   several

2. two of something   _5_   none

3. more than two of something _1_   single

4. a multitude of something   _4_   many

5. the absence of anything   _2_   pair

B. Write *T* or *F* in each blank.   Change false statements to make them true.

_T_   1. Very young children should never cross a street alone.

_F_   2. Stars shine brightly during the day.   **The sun shines during the day.**

C. Circle the correct answer.

1. Louisiana is _____.

   ~~a.~~ in the southern part of the United States
   b.   a state which grows sugar cane
   c.   located on Lake Erie
   (d.) both a and b

2. Christmas is _____.

   (a.) a special holiday
   b.   a religion
   c.   a man's name
   d.   none of the above

D. Use the following words to complete each statement.   Each word may be used only once.

particle   flask   fodder

1. Food for farm animals is *fodder* .

2. A *flask* is a glass or metal bottle.

3. A small speck or spot is called a ~~*fodder*~~ **particle** .

E. Essay

Describe a close friend, using at least five adjectives.   The adjectives should tell the qualities you most enjoy or appreciate.

I have a very close friend who listens to whatever I have to say. My friend is very kind and generous with time.

She is nice to everyone and fun to be with.   Most of all, I appreciate her good

sense of humor.

Worksheet: *The Final Proof*

Finally, the last worksheet allows your students to correct their own mistakes. By retaking a previous test, your students can improve their performance and proof a test with confidence. The worksheet provides a checklist for your students to follow.

The Final Proof Name _____

All the proof is in! Your teacher will give you a test which you have already taken. Now, take the test again, and proof it. Use the sentence guide below to make sure you didn't forget anything. Check each item below as you proof your test.

____ 1. I followed the directions, by marking them and noting important words.

____ 2. I didn't leave any blanks, unless I left them for a reason.

____ 3. I checked the test for right answers. I looked at the test in a different order than when I took it.

____ 4. I rewrote answers and compared them to my first answers.

When you have finished proofing your test, talk about what parts of the proofing helped you the most. Did you get a different or higher grade with the corrections? Do you think proofing is worth the time it takes? What does proofing prove to you?

WORKSHEET 136 Copyright© 1987 LinguiSystems, Inc.

7 Ways to Proofread Your Tests

Name _____

Detectives solve crimes with <u>proof</u> or facts. You can find proof about how you did on a test by proofreading it. Proofing can also help you find that you might have skipped problems, were incomplete in answering, did not follow directions, or answered incorrectly.

Let's see how to proofread a test to catch your mistakes. Here's what you do when you've finished your test.

119 Reread the directions for each section of the test. Be sure you have followed the directions.

120 Next, look over the entire test. Be sure you have finished all answers you wanted to answer.

121 Now, check your answers. Look at the test as if you had never seen it before.

122 To check your answers, cover your answers with your hand and answer the questions again. Check to see if you agree with the answer you wrote the first time.

123 Review the test in a different order from the order you took it in. For example, proof the test from back to front.

124 If you have time, try to rewrite your answers. Rewriting the answers helps you be sure you didn't leave out anything or give any wrong information.

125 In math, do some special test-proofing. Check multiplication with division and check subtraction with addition.

Problem	43	Check	$3\overline{)129}$ 43		Problem	47	Check	19

$$\begin{array}{r} 43 \\ \times\ 3 \\ \hline 129 \end{array} \qquad 3\overline{)129}^{\;43} \qquad\qquad \begin{array}{r} 47 \\ -19 \\ \hline 28 \end{array} \qquad \begin{array}{r} 19 \\ +28 \\ \hline 47 \end{array}$$

Let's see some proofing in action. You had a matching test that you answered like this:

3	Pacific Ocean	1.	U.S. northern border
4	Atlantic Ocean	2.	U.S. southern border
1	Canada	3.	U.S. western border
4	Gulf of Mexico	4.	U.S. eastern border

By proofing, you see that you used number 4 twice.   Reread the questions to see which answer is 4.   Do you think it might have helped to cross out the numbers as you used them?

You had a true-false test which you answered like this:

Directions: Write *T* or *F* in the blank.   Change false statements to true ones.

___F___   Maine is a southeastern state.

By proofing for direction-following, you realize you did not change the false statement to a true one.   You know Maine isn't in the Southeast.   You write *northern* above the wrong part of the statement, like this:

                    northern
___F___   Maine is a southeastern state.

Perhaps you could have numbered the parts of the directions to be sure you followed all the parts.

You had a multiple-choice question you answered like this:

Directions: Circle the correct number for each answer.

A carnival is _____.

⊗ a celebration
2. a sorrowful time
3. a festival
④ both 1 and 3

By proofing or rereading the question, you realize that you must have stopped reading after number 1.   Since number 3 is also correct, your answer is number 4.   You go back and erase your wrong answer or cross it out.

You wrote an essay answer like this:

Name and describe two forms of dance.

Ballet
Jazz

By proofing, you realize that you only <u>named</u> two forms of dance.   You should have <u>described</u> them, too.   Maybe you could have marked part of the direction like this:

<u>Name</u> and <u>describe</u> two forms of dance.

By underlining different parts of the question, you help yourself remember to answer all the parts of the question.   Good thing you caught your mistake, right?

131

Check-a-Test

Do you think you're ready to prove how much you've learned?   Suppose that you have just finished this test.   Now, check your work.   Correct your mistakes.

A.   List five characteristics of your school.   Each characteristic should be an adjective.

1. big
2. noisy
3. cold
4. I have friends there
5. friendly

B.   Write *T* for True or *F* for False in each blank.   Make true statements false.

_____T_____   1.   The sun is a star.

_____T_____   2.   Air conditioners help keep us cool.

C.   Write the number of the definition in the blank next to the correct word.

1.   coldest season   ___1___ winter

2.   leaves turn color   ___4___ spring

3.   hottest season   ___3___ summer

4.   plants bloom again   ___4___ fall

D.   Use the following word to complete each statement.   Each word may be used more than once.

              infants   children   adults

1.   People who usually make rules are ___adults___.

2.   People most likely to be in school are children.

3.   People who usually go to work each day are Infants.

4.   People who most often make their needs known by crying are infants.

5.   People who spend most of their time playing are infants.

132

E. Explain the reasons for the Civil War.   Write at least three sentences.

The Civil War was fought over the idea of slavery.

_____

_____

_____

_____

F. Do you think twelve years of school is enough, too little, or too much?   Tell why you feel as you do in at least three or four sentences.

Yes. _____

_____

_____

_____

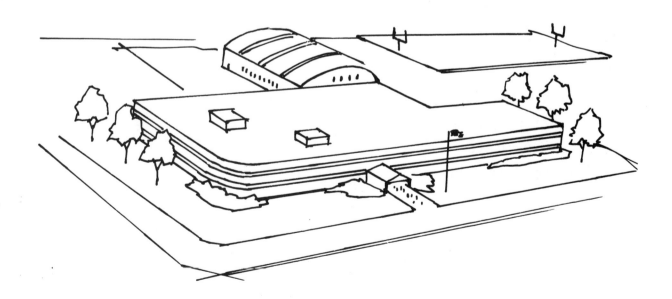

The Proof Is in the Answers

Name _____

You're almost ready to try the real thing. Let's proof one more time! Suppose you have just finished this test. Now, check your work. Correct your mistakes.

A. Write the letter of the definition that matches each word.

1. one of anything   _4_   several

2. two of something   _5_   none

3. more than two of something _1_   single

4. a multitude of something   _4_   many

5. the absence of anything   _2_   pair

B. Write *T* or *F* in each blank.   Change false statements to make them true.

_T_ 1. Very young children should never cross a street alone.

_F_ 2. Stars shine brightly during the day.

C. Circle the correct answer.

1. Louisiana is _____.

   (a.) in the southern part of the United States
    b.   a state which grows sugar cane
    c.   located on Lake Erie
    d.   both a and b

2. Christmas is _____.

   (a.) a special holiday
    b.   a religion
    c.   a man's name
    d.   none of the above

The Proof Is in the Answers, continued

Name _____

D. Use the following words to complete each statement. Each word may be used only once.

particle   flask   fodder

1. Food for farm animals is _fodder_.

2. A _flask_ is a glass or metal bottle.

3. A small speck or spot is called a _particle_.

E. Essay

Describe a close friend, using at least five adjectives. The adjectives should tell the qualities you most enjoy or appreciate.

I have a very close friend who listens to
whatever I have to say. My friend is very kind
and generous with time.

The Final Proof

Name _____

All the proof is in!   Your teacher will give you a test which you have already taken.   Now, take the test again, and proof it.   Use the sentence guide below to make sure you didn't forget anything.   Check each item below as you proof your test.

_____ 1.   I followed the directions, by marking them and noting important words.

_____ 2.   I didn't leave any blanks, unless I left them for a reason.

_____ 3.   I checked the test for right answers.   I looked at the test in a different order than when I took it.

_____ 4.   I rewrote answers and compared them to my first answers.

When you have finished proofing your test, talk about what parts of the proofing helped you the most.   Did you get a different or higher grade with the corrections?   Do you think proofing is worth the time it takes?   What does proofing prove to you?

1-2-123467